BIBLE STORIES FOR EXHAUSTED WOMEN

IMMERSIVE RETELLINGS TO QUIET RACING
THOUGHTS, RELEASE HEAVY BURDENS, AND
FALL ASLEEP IN PEACE WITHOUT THE
PRESSURE TO STUDY

ZOE LAMB

Scripture Notice: Scripture references appear at the beginning of each chapter. The biblical language throughout this book is paraphrased in the author's own words for readability and devotional flow. These paraphrases are not quoted from, and are not intended to replace, any single Bible translation. Readers are encouraged to consult the Bible in their preferred translation for the complete text of each passage.

Disclaimer: This book is provided for inspirational and devotional purposes only. It is not intended as, and should not be considered a substitute for, pastoral care, spiritual direction, professional counseling, medical advice, mental health treatment, or crisis support. If you are experiencing persistent distress, anxiety, depression, or sleep disruption, or if you need immediate help, please seek support from a qualified pastor, licensed professional, healthcare provider, or local emergency services.

CONTENTS

INTRODUCTION

If you are here right now, reading or listening, there is a good chance you are tired.

I do not mean the kind of tired that is fixed by one night of sleeping in or a last-minute weekend away. I mean the deep, marrow-level exhaustion that settles into your bones after you have been strong for too long.

Maybe you are the woman who keeps track of everything for your entire family. You know where the shin guards are, when the insurance bill is due, and which child is a little more fragile today. You carry the invisible load of emotional management, smoothing over conflicts before they start and absorbing the stress of the people you love so they do not have to feel it.

Maybe you are the woman who feels like she is constantly running on a treadmill that is moving just a little too fast. You wake up with a racing heart, your mind already scrolling through a to-do list that feels impossible before your feet even hit the floor. You spend your days putting out fires, answering emails, and serving others, only to collapse into bed at night wondering if you did enough.

Or maybe you are the woman who feels spiritually dry. You love God, or you want to, but the thought of opening your Bible feels like just another chore. You see the social media posts of perfectly highlighted Bibles and steaming mugs of coffee, and you feel a pang of guilt because your quiet time has been distracted or nonexistent. You worry that God is disappointed in you. You worry that your exhaustion is a sign of a lack of faith.

If any of that resonates with you, I want you to take a deep breath. Right now.

Inhale.

Exhale.

You are not failing. You are just carrying a lot. And you have come to the right place.

The Lie of "Doing It All"

Somewhere along the way, we bought into a lie. It was a subtle one, wrapped in good intentions and even Bible verses. We were told that to be a godly woman meant to be a machine of productivity.

We looked at the Proverbs 31 woman, an ancient poem meant to celebrate the valor of a woman, and we turned her into a modern checklist. We convinced ourselves that if we are not rising while it is still night, running a business, raising perfect children, and volunteering for every cause, we are somehow falling short of God's design.

We started believing that the love of God is a salary we earn, rather than a gift we receive. We started believing that rest is a reward for finishing the work, rather than a rhythm designed by the Creator.

But here is the truth: the work is never finished. There will always be another dish to wash, another email to answer, and another crisis to solve. If you wait until you are done to rest, you will never rest.

And here is the deeper truth: God does not love you because you are productive. He does not love you because you are the first one up or the last one down. He does not love you because of your color-coded Bible study notes or your volunteer hours.

He loved you before you did a single thing. He loved you while you were still in your mother's womb, when He was already forming and knowing you, before you had a to-do list, before you had a title, and before you had a reputation to maintain.

You are human. You were made from dust. You were designed with limits. The beautiful, scandalous news of the Gospel is that God meets us in our limits, not after we overcome them.

A Sanctuary, Not a Study

This book is different from the other books on your nightstand.

This is not a Bible study. There are no fill-in-the-blank questions here. There is no Greek word of the day to memorize. There are no three steps to a better life that you need to implement tomorrow morning. You have enough work to do. You do not need your time with God to feel like another job.

Instead, think of this book as a sanctuary. Think of it as a soft place to land.

In these pages, we are going to revisit the stories of women in the Bible. But we are not going to analyze them for theology or extract moral lessons on how to be better. We are going to step into their sandals.

We are going to sit in the dust with Hagar and feel the heat of the desert sun. We are going to feel the weight of the water jar on the shoulder of the woman at the well. We are going to feel the ache in the throat of Hannah as she tries to pray through her tears.

We are going to find that the women of the Bible were not stained-glass saints with perfect halos. They were real, messy women. They were exhausted, afraid, misunderstood, overworked, and grieving.

In every single story, we will find that God did not ask them to try harder. He did not lecture them on their lack of faith. He did not give them a performance review. He met them. He sat with them. He fed them. He listened to them.

How to Use This Book

I have a very specific request for how you use this book. Please, do not study it. Do not read this with a highlighter in your hand, looking for profound quotes to remember. Do not listen to the audiobook thinking you need to pause, rewind, or take notes to get something out of it.

I want you to use this book as a way to power down.

Read one chapter at night, perhaps when the house is finally quiet. Or listen to one chapter as you lie in bed. Let the story wash over you. Picture yourself in the scene. Smell the air, hear the sounds, and feel the emotions. Let your brain switch from analysis mode to story mode.

Each chapter begins with two sections. "The Immersion" invites you to settle into the specific Bible story and step into the world of the woman at the center of it, so you can experience the scene and her emotions without rushing. "The Connection" then gently brings the story into your own life, helping you notice where you may be carrying similar burdens, questions, or weariness.

If you fall asleep while reading, good. That is a spiritual victory. If you cry, let the tears come. That is a form of prayer. If you get to the end of a chapter and the only thing you can say is, "Thank you, God, that you see me," then you have done enough.

At the end of each chapter, you will find a section called "The Release." It is a simple truth to hold onto. Then you will find "The Invitation," a tiny, low-effort way to connect with God that requires zero energy. And finally, a "Bedtime Prayer," a short prayer to whisper into the dark before you close your eyes.

Your Permission Slip

The world will tell you that you need to earn your rest. It will tell you that rest is for the weak, the lazy, or the finished.

But the Creator of the Universe rested. And He invites you to do the same. So, consider this introduction your official permission slip.

You have permission to stop, even if the house is messy. You have permission to say no, even if it disappoints someone. You have permission to be weak, even if everyone relies on your strength. You have permission to let God hold the world for a while.

The day is done. The striving can cease. You are safe here.

Let us begin.

A Note About Scripture

At the start of each chapter, you will see the Bible passages the story is drawn from. The story language is intentionally paraphrased so you can rest and receive the message without the pressure to study or remember every verse. If you would like the exact wording, you can open your Bible to those verses in the translation you trust and love.

PART I

THE EXHAUSTION
OF STRIVING

Stories for when you feel like you aren't "enough."

We start here because this is where most of us live. We live in the gap between who we are and who we think we should be. We strive to be more lovable, more productive, and more put-together. We treat the love of God like a transaction we must complete, rather than a gift we simply open.

In this section, we meet three women who tried to work for their worth. We will watch them hustle, hide, and burn out until they collide with the God who asked them to stop.

1

THE EXHAUSTION OF TRYING TO EARN LOVE

THE STORY OF LEAH (GENESIS 29:1-35)

T he Weight of Being Second Best

There is a specific kind of tiredness that settles in the bones of a woman who feels she is "Option B."

It is not just physical fatigue, though it certainly makes your limbs feel heavy. It is a spiritual heaviness. It is the exhaustion of walking into a room and scanning the faces of the people there, wondering if anyone is actually happy to see you, or if they are just tolerating your presence. It is the exhaustion of over-explaining yourself, of laughing a little too loud to be noticed, or of saying "yes" to favors you do not have the energy to do, simply because you are terrified that if you say "no," you will be replaced.

It is the exhaustion of the transactional heart.

Somewhere along the way, many of us picked up a silent equation. We learned it on playgrounds, in classrooms, and sometimes, tragically, in our own homes. The equation goes like this: I am lovable only if I am useful. I am valuable only if I am impressive. I am chosen only if I am perfect.

So we begin the hustle. We work for affection. We polish our personalities until they shine. We hide our needs because needy people are inconvenient, and inconvenient people get left behind. We become the "low-maintenance" friend, the "easy-going" wife, or the "reliable" daughter. We convince ourselves that if we can just perform well enough, we will finally secure our place.

But deep down, in the quiet moments before sleep takes us, the fear whispers: "If I stopped trying, would anyone stay?"

If you are nodding your head, if your chest feels tight just reading those words, I want you to know that you are not the first woman to feel this. You are part of a long lineage of women who have tried to hustle for their worth.

And the matriarch of this lineage, the woman who knows this pain more intimately than anyone else in Scripture, is a woman named Leah.

Tonight, we are going to go back to her tent. We are going to sit with her in the dust. And we are going to watch what happens when a woman finally stops trying to earn a love that cannot be bought, and instead falls into the arms of a Love that was hers all along.

THE IMMERSION

Let the world fade away now. Let the noise of your day, the traffic, the notifications, and the demands, dissolve into the silence of the desert.

Imagine the air is cooling down. The sun has dipped below the horizon, painting the sky in streaks of purple and deep indigo. You can smell the scent of wool, of woodsmoke from the campfires, and the dry, ancient dust of Haran.

You are Leah.

And you are invisible.

You have lived your entire life in the shadow of your younger sister, Rachel. The Bible tells us that Rachel was beautiful in both appearance and figure. She was the kind of woman who stopped conversation when she walked into a room. She was sparkling, vivacious, and the main character in everyone's story.

But you? The text describes you with one cryptic phrase: "Leah was tender eyed." Some translators say this meant they were crossed, or gentle, or lacking fire. But in the harsh economy of the ancient world, it meant simply this: You were not the prize. You were the background character. You were the one people looked past to get a glimpse of your sister.

You grew up knowing that you were the difficult daughter to marry off. You absorbed the disappointment of your father. You learned to be quiet, to be small, and to stay out of the way.

But then, Jacob came.

You watched him from the shadows of the tent flaps. You saw the way his face softened when he first looked at Rachel by the well, how emotion overtook him at the sight of her. You watched him labor for seven long years for her hand, years that passed quickly to him because of the depth of his love for her.

Can you imagine the ache of watching that kind of love from the outside? Witnessing a romance that you are excluded from? You watched your sister be chosen, cherished, and adored, while you remained in the gray twilight of being "the other one."

And then came the night of the betrayal.

Your father is a man who loves money more than he loves his daughters. He hatches a plan. He knows no one has offered for you. He knows Jacob is a worker he wants to keep. So he treats you not as a daughter, but as currency.

He tells you the plan: Tonight, under the cover of darkness, under the heavy veil of the bride, you will go into the tent of Jacob. You will take the place of your sister.

Imagine the humiliation. Imagine the protest rising in your throat, dying before it reaches your lips because in this world, you do not have a voice.

So, you are dressed in the finery of your sister. You are draped in the heavy, opaque veil. You are walked across the camp in the dark.

Your heart is hammering against your ribs, not with the excitement of a bride, but with the terror of an imposter. You know that the man waiting in that tent does not want you. You know that every tender word he whispers in the dark is meant for someone else. You are stealing a life that does not belong to you.

The night passes in a blur of shame and silence. You cannot speak, or he will know the voice. You cannot show your face. You have to hide, even in the most intimate act of marriage.

And then, the sun rises.

This is the moment that has haunted your nightmares. The light creeps into the tent. It illuminates the rugs, the clay jars, and finally, your face.

Jacob opens his eyes. He turns to smile at his beloved Rachel, the woman he has worked seven years for.

And instead, he sees you.

Scripture does not record the dialogue, but we can sense the recoil. We can feel the shock, the confusion, and then the crushing realization. Later, he confronts your father in anguish, demanding how this could have been done to him.

But in that moment, in the silence of the tent, you see the look in his eyes. It is not love. It is not even kindness. It is horror. It is disappointment.

To be seen, fully and truly, and to see disappointment in the eyes of the person looking at you, that is a wound that goes deeper than bone. It confirms your worst fear: I am not enough. I am not the one he wanted.

Jacob storms out. He marries Rachel a week later. And you are left in the tent, a wife in title, but a widow in heart. You are part of the household, but not part of the love story.

Now, the exhaustion truly begins.

Because you decide, in your grief, that you can fix this. You decide that if you cannot be the beautiful wife, you will be the productive wife. You will work harder than Rachel. You will give him what Rachel cannot. You will buy his heart with your body.

You become pregnant. Hope flares in your chest like a desperate flame. Surely, you think, surely a son will make him look at me with affection.

You give birth to a baby boy and name him Reuben. His name means "the Lord has seen my affliction, and now my husband will love me."

Do you hear the plea in that name? It is not just a name; it is a bargain. It is a message sent across the camp to Jacob. "Look. I gave you a firstborn. I did a good job. Love me now?"

But the text implies nothing changed. The eyes of Jacob remained fixed on Rachel.

So, you try again. You grit your teeth. You endure the pregnancy, the labor, and the long nights of nursing. You bear another son. You name him Simeon, which means "the Lord has heard that I was hated."

The first name was a hope; this second name is a statement of fact. "I am not loved." It is a public declaration of your loneliness. You are shouting your pain, naming it, and putting it on the birth certificate of your child, hoping someone, anyone, will listen.

Still, Jacob is distant. He is polite, perhaps. Dutiful. But his heart is in the other tent.

So you double down. You work harder. You try for a third time. If one son did not do it, and two did not do it, maybe three is the magic number. Maybe three makes a pattern. Maybe three makes a family.

You give birth to Levi, and this time the name feels heartbreakingly specific. Levi means "attached" or "joined." You name him with the hope that now your husband will finally be joined to you, because you have borne him three sons.

Can you feel the exhaustion in that "now this time"? You are bargaining for connection. You are thinking, "I have done everything right. I have checked every box. I have been fertile, faithful, and productive. I have earned this. Why is it not working?"

Imagine Leah at this stage. She is tired. Her body is worn from three back-to-back pregnancies. Her emotional well is dry. She has spent years hustling for a gaze that never lingers on her. She has tried to perform her way into intimacy, and she has found that performance is a currency that has no value in the economy of love.

She is empty. She has nothing left to give.

And it is right there, at the end of her striving, at the bottom of her hope, that everything changes.

THE CONNECTION

Let us step out of the tent for a moment and come back to the present.

You might not be competing with a sister for a husband. You might not be naming children as cries for help. But I know you know the hustle of Leah.

I know you know what it feels like to think: "Now at last."

"Now that I have lost the twenty pounds, at last I can be confident."

"Now that I have been promoted, at last I can feel secure."

"Now that I have reorganized the entire house and made it look like a magazine, at last my mother-in-law will respect me."

"Now that I have fixed all the problems of my husband, at last he will be emotionally available."

We live our lives on the treadmill of "If/Then." If I do enough, then I will be enough. If I am useful, then I will be kept.

This is the exhaustion of the woman who is terrified of being a burden. You are the one who never asks for help. You are the one who apologizes for taking up space. You are the one who over-functions in every relationship, doing the planning, the remembering, and the fixing, because you secretly believe that your value lies in your output.

You believe that if you stopped working, the relationship would die, because you are the only one holding the rope.

And just like Leah, you are finding that it does not work. The promotion comes, but the imposter syndrome stays. The weight is lost, but the self-criticism remains. The house is clean, but the marriage is still messy.

You are pleading to be seen, heard, and chosen with everything you do, but the world just takes what you give and asks for more.

It is exhausting to be Leah. It is exhausting to live as if love is a paycheck. It burns you out. It dries up your soul. It keeps you awake at 3:00 AM, tallying up your failures and wondering why, after all this effort, you still feel so incredibly lonely.

You are tired because you are doing a job you were never meant to do. You are trying to justify your own existence.

THE RELEASE

Let us go back to Leah.

She has birthed three sons. She has spent years looking horizontally, looking across the tent at Jacob, waiting for him to validate her. She has been desperate for a man to give her a soul.

She becomes pregnant a fourth time.

The weeks pass. Her belly swells. The familiar ache of her back returns. But something is happening in her spirit. The silence in the tent is no longer terrifying; it is becoming a sanctuary.

She realizes that Jacob is never going to give her what she needs. The well of his heart is dry for her. She cannot work hard enough to make him love her.

She hits the wall. She gives up.

And in that surrender, she finds something else.

She gives birth to her fourth son. She holds him in her arms. She looks at his small face, his closed eyes, and his tiny hands.

And for the first time, she does not mention Jacob.

She does not say, "Maybe my husband will love me." She does not say, "Now I will be appreciated."

She lifts her head. She looks past Jacob, past Rachel, past the tent ceiling, and past the stars. She looks into the face of the God who has been with her in the dark every single night.

She names the baby Judah.

And Judah means: "Now I will praise the Lord."

Do you feel the weight falling off her shoulders? She stops asking, "Do you love me?" to a man, and she starts saying, "I praise You" to

God. She shifts her gaze from the lack in her life to the abundance of her Creator. She stops striving. She retires from the business of earning love. She simply accepts her place as a mother, a woman, and a daughter of God.

Here is The Release for you tonight.

God did not wait for Leah to be loved by Jacob before He blessed her.

God did not say, "Leah, once you fix your marriage, then I will use you." God saw her in her unchosen state. He saw her tender eyes and her broken heart. And He said, "I can build a kingdom with that."

Because here is the twist in the story, the twist that Leah herself did not live to fully understand, but one that we can see now.

Jacob loved Rachel. Rachel was the beauty. Rachel was the romance. But God chose Leah.

From Leah came Levi, the tribe of the priests. Every priest who ever entered the Holy of Holies to make intercession for the people came from the womb of the unloved wife.

And from Leah came Judah, the tribe of the kings. King David, the man after God's own heart, was a descendant of Leah. Solomon, the wisest man on earth, was a descendant of Leah.

And generations later, in a stable in Bethlehem, a baby cried out in the night. Jesus. The Lion of the Tribe of Judah.

The Savior of the world did not come from the line of the beautiful, sparkling, lovable Rachel. He came from the line of Leah, the woman who was tired, the woman who was ignored, and the woman who had to learn to praise God in the dark.

God does not need you to be the "Main Character." He does not need you to be the sparkly one. He does not need you to be the one everyone applauds.

He loves the tired one. He chooses the one who has stopped trying to impress Him.

Leah thought she was Option B. But in the redemptive plan of God, she was Option A all along.

You do not have to earn this. You could not earn it if you tried. You are part of the family not because of what you produce, but because of who you belong to.

THE INVITATION

You have been holding the rope for a long time.

You know the rope I am talking about. It is that mental tug-of-war you are playing with someone, or maybe with the world in general. The rope represents your need for approval. You are pulling and pulling, your knuckles white, and your muscles shaking, terrified that if you let go, you will fall. You think that holding this tension is the only thing keeping you safe.

But tonight, we are going to do what Leah did with Judah. We are going to drop the rope.

This is a low-effort visualization. You do not have to move your body. You just have to use your imagination.

The "Drop the Rope" Visualization

Close your eyes. If you are lying in bed, let your shoulders sink into the mattress. Unclench your jaw. Remove your tongue from the roof of your mouth.

1. **Picture the rope.** Imagine you are holding a thick, heavy rope in your hands. On the other end of the rope is the thing you are trying to earn. Maybe it is the approval of a parent. Maybe it is the forgiveness of a friend. Maybe it is the feeling of being "good enough."

2. **Feel the tension.** Notice how tired your arms are. Notice how much energy it takes to keep this rope taut. You have been pulling for years.

3. **Visualize the release.** In the eye of your mind, look at your hands. They are cramped around the rope. Now, slowly, watch your fingers open. One by one. Pinky finger. Ring finger. Middle finger. Index finger. Thumb.

4. **Watch it fall.** See the rope slip from your palms and hit the ground. Thud.

5. **Notice what happens.** You did not fall over. The world did not end. You are still standing. You are standing on solid ground. You are free.

You do not have to pull anymore. You can just be.

BEDTIME PRAYER

We end this chapter not with a to-do list, but with a prayer. A few words to whisper to your soul as you drift off. You can say them out loud, or simply hold them in the quiet of your mind.

God of Leah,

I come to You tired of earning. Tired of measuring myself. Tired of auditing my worth and searching the mirror for proof that I am enough.

Tonight, I lay that burden down. I step out of the role of justifying my existence. I confess that I cannot buy Your love, and I thank You that Your love is not for sale.

Like Leah, turn my eyes away from what I lack and toward who You are. Teach my heart to rest in what You have already spoken over me. Quiet the voice that says I must prove myself to be safe, to be chosen, to be loved.

Remind me that I am not a servant trying to earn a wage. I am Your daughter, already welcomed, already held, already home.

So I place my work in Your hands. I release the outcomes I cannot control. I release the people I cannot fix. I release the expectations I cannot meet. You are holding the world, and You are holding me.

Let sleep come as a gift, not a reward. Cover me with Your peace. Let my body unclench. Let my mind grow still. Speak over me what is true. I am seen. I am heard. I am loved.

Amen.

2

THE EXHAUSTION OF DOING IT ALL

THE STORY OF MARTHA (LUKE 10:38-42)

The Weight of the Invisible Load

There is a role in every family, every office, and every friend group that comes with a heavy, invisible crown. It is the role of the "Responsible One."

If you are reading or listening to this book, I suspect you are wearing that crown right now.

You are the one who knows where the birth certificates are filed. You are the one who remembers the dog needs heartworm medicine on the first of the month. You are the one who notices the milk is running low, the permission slip needs a signature, and your father-in-law's birthday is three weeks away (and you have already bought the card).

You are the Project Manager of your universe.

While the world often praises you for being "so organized" or "so capable," people rarely see the cost. They do not see the running ticker tape in your mind that never shuts off. Even when you are sitting on the couch, supposedly relaxing, you are mentally calculating how long the laundry has been in the washer and whether you remembered to reply to that text message.

This is the exhaustion of the "mental load."

It is different from physical tiredness. You can sleep for ten hours and still wake up exhausted because your brain has been working the night shift, categorizing worries and scheduling the future.

There is a specific kind of resentment that grows in the soil of this exhaustion. It is a hot, quiet anger. It bubbles up when you see others relaxing. You watch your husband sit down to watch a football game, or your children play video games, or your friends laugh over coffee without a care in the world, and you want to scream: "Do you not see what needs to be done? Do you think this house cleans itself? Do you think dinner appears by magic?"

But you do not scream. You just work harder. You sigh louder. You clang the dishes a little more forcefully, hoping someone will notice the martyrdom in your movement and come to rescue you.

But they usually do not. They just think you are in a bad mood.

This dynamic, involving the over-functioning woman and the under-functioning world around her, is not a modern invention. It did not start with Google calendars or smartphones. It is an ancient struggle.

Tonight, we are going to visit the patron saint of the overwhelmed. We are going to step into the kitchen of a woman named Martha, who felt like the only adult in the room, and see how Jesus handled her heavy heart.

THE IMMERSION

Let's go to Bethany.

It is a small village, just a few miles from Jerusalem. It is a dusty, humble place, but tonight, there is an electricity in the air. The Rabbi is coming.

Jesus of Nazareth is the Healer and the Teacher. He is the man who turns water into wine and despair into hope. He is not just passing through; He is coming to your house.

You are Martha, and you are the mistress of this home.

This is not a casual drop-in. In this culture, hospitality is not a hobby; it is a sacred duty. It is a matter of honor and shame. To host a Rabbi means to feed him, but not just him. He travels with twelve men. Thirteen hungry, dusty travelers are currently crowding into your main room.

Imagine the sheer logistics of this moment.

You are in the kitchen area, which is not a separate room with a door you can close, but a space adjacent to the gathering, separated perhaps by an archway or a curtain. You can hear them. You can hear the low rumble of their voices, the laughter, and the scraping of sandals against the stone floor.

But you cannot join them. You are too busy ensuring they are comfortable.

Feel the heat of the fire on your face. You are bent over the hearth, stirring a stew that needs to be perfect. The air is thick with the smell of roasting meat, baking bread, and woodsmoke. Sweat is trickling down your spine, soaking into your tunic. Your hair is sticking to your forehead.

Your hands are moving fast, chopping herbs, kneading dough, and pouring wine. Your mind is moving even faster. Do we have enough cups? Did I soak the lentils long enough? Is the fire dying down? Why is it so hot in here?

Your feet ache. You have been standing since sunrise, prepping for this moment. You want everything to be perfect for Jesus. You love Him. You want to serve Him. You want to show Him how much you honor Him by the quality of your table.

As the minutes tick by, the joy of service begins to curdle into something else.

You glance through the doorway into the cool, shadowed living area.

There they are. The men are reclining. They look relaxed. They are listening to Jesus speak. The atmosphere is peaceful, reverent, and calm.

And there, sitting right at the feet of Jesus in the spot reserved for a disciple, is your sister Mary.

She is not carrying a pitcher. She is not checking the bread. She is not looking at you to see if you need help. She is sitting there, hands empty and eyes fixed on Jesus, as if the world has stopped turning. It is as if hunger does not exist. It is as if you do not exist.

The resentment hits you like a physical blow to the stomach.

It starts as a thought: "Does she not care?" Then it becomes an accusation: "She is lazy. She is selfish. She is leaving it all to me." Finally, it turns toward the Guest of Honor: "Why is He letting her do this? Does He not see me sweating in here? Does He not appreciate the work it takes to feed Him?"

The clang of the pots gets louder. You slam a bowl down, hoping Mary will flinch and realize her error. She does not.

The narrative of self-pity begins to spin in your head, gaining speed with every rotation. "I am the only one who cares. I am the only one who works. I am alone."

Finally, the pressure in your chest becomes too much to contain. The stew boils over, and so do you.

You wipe your hands on your apron. You march out of the kitchen, your face flushed and your breathing shallow. You walk right into the middle of the teaching. You interrupt the Son of God.

You do not look at Mary. You look straight at Jesus, and the words come out sharp and raw, the way they do when you have been holding it in too long. You tell Him your sister has left you to carry all the work alone. You ask if He even sees it, if He even cares. And then you say the line you have been rehearsing in your mind: "Tell her to come help me."

You stand there, chest heaving, waiting for the vindication. You are waiting for someone to finally acknowledge how hard you are working.

THE CONNECTION

Let's leave the stone floor of Bethany and come back to your life.

We are often hard on Martha. In sermons, she is frequently painted as the villain, the distracted, grumpy antithesis to the holy, spiritual Mary. But I want to defend Martha for a moment. I want to defend you.

Martha was not doing anything wrong. She was doing something necessary. People have to eat. If Martha sat down, everyone would go hungry.

This is the trap of the "Responsible Woman." You are not doing frivolous things. You are doing essential things. You are paying the bills so the lights stay on. You are doing the laundry so the kids have clean clothes. You are cooking the dinner so bodies are nourished. You are managing the emotions of your household so that everyone feels safe.

The exhaustion comes not from the tasks themselves, but from the feeling that you are the only barrier between order and chaos.

You believe that if you stop spinning the plates, they will all crash, and it will be your fault.

Like Martha, your resentment often targets the people who seem to have stopped carrying their share. You resent your husband for sitting down when the kitchen is messy. You resent your friend who takes a weekend trip while you are catching up on work. You resent the people who seem to have given themselves permission to rest, while you are still waiting for someone to give you permission.

But be honest: there is also a dark kind of pride in it, is there not?

We wear our exhaustion like a badge of honor. When people ask, "How are you?" we say, "Oh, just so busy. Crazy busy." We want them to know. We want credit for the sacrifice. We want to be the hero of the story, the one who carries the world on her back.

But the cost of being the hero is that you are lonely.

You are "distracted," as the Bible says. Drawn away. Pulled in a dozen directions at once.

And that is exactly how it feels, is it not? You are spinning. You are being dragged from task to task to task. You are physically present in the room with your family, but your mind is elsewhere under the weight of the mental load. You are serving everyone, but you are connecting with no one.

You are standing in the kitchen, furious and lonely, while the very Peace you are serving is sitting in the other room, waiting for you.

THE RELEASE

Let's go back to the moment of confrontation.

Martha has just blurted out her demand. Tell her to help me.

The room goes quiet. You can almost feel everyone freeze. The disciples probably look down, suddenly fascinated by the floor. The tension is thick, sharp, and public.

Jesus looks at Martha.

He sees the sweat. He sees the flour on her hands. He sees the tightness in her jaw, the panic behind her eyes, the exhaustion that has curdled into anger.

And He does not scold her.

He does not shame her for caring about the meal. He does not dismiss her feelings. He does not tell her to calm down and stop making a scene.

He says her name. Twice.

"Martha. Martha."

Not as a slap, but as a reaching. A steadying. The way someone speaks when they want you to come back to yourself. He holds her gaze long enough to slow her spinning thoughts. He presses pause on the frantic inner noise.

Then He tells her the truth with tenderness. You are pulled in too many directions. You are carrying too much. You are anxious and weighed down by many things. But only one thing is truly necessary, and Mary has chosen it, and it will not be taken from her.

This is the release.

Jesus is telling Martha, and He is telling you, that the standard you have set for yourself is not His standard.

Martha thought the necessary thing was excellence. A full spread. A perfectly swept floor. A flawless performance as the capable host. Jesus says, that is not what I needed. A simple meal would have been enough. Bread and something small. I did not come for the food. I came for you.

He is giving her permission to lower the bar.

He is showing her that she has built a cage out of expectations, and then exhausted herself trying to live inside it. And He is inviting her to step out.

When He says Mary has chosen the better portion, He is not condemning service. Jesus served His whole life. He washed feet. He fed crowds. He touched the untouchable. Service is not the problem.

Striving is.

The kind of striving that believes love must be earned. The kind that turns devotion into performance. The kind that works itself into the ground and calls it faithfulness.

The one thing that is necessary is being with Him. Receiving. Letting your soul sit down in His presence without trying to prove it deserves to be there.

Martha thought she was the host and Jesus was the guest. But in the kingdom of God, Jesus is always the Host. We are the guests. We are the hungry ones. We are the ones who need to be fed.

Martha was trying to give God something He did not require, at the expense of the one thing He wanted, her heart.

Here is the radical permission Jesus offers you tonight. The world will not fall apart if you sit down.

If the laundry piles up, let it. If dinner is frozen pizza instead of homemade, let it be frozen. If the email waits until tomorrow, let it wait.

You are allowed to step over the mess to sit at His feet. You are allowed to disappoint expectations in order to preserve your own soul. You are allowed to stop hosting and start being held.

Mary's portion, the portion of rest, of listening, of being near to Him, cannot be taken away. The dishes will be taken away. The clean house will get dirty again. The to-do list will regenerate. But the rest you find in Jesus is not fragile. It is not temporary. It is yours to keep.

THE INVITATION

You might be thinking, "That sounds nice, but I have a job. I have kids. I can't just sit at anyone's feet all day."

I know. You cannot resign from your life. But you can resign from the pressure to do it all perfectly. You can resign from the mental load of trying to be the savior of your family.

We are going to do a very small, practical exercise. It takes two minutes.

The "One Thing" Audit

1. **Visualize Tomorrow.** Think about the day ahead of you. Think about that to-do list scrolling in your head. It probably has 10, 15, or 20 items on it.
2. **Pick Three.** If you could only do three things tomorrow—if you physically could not do a fourth—what would the absolute essentials be? (e.g., Feed the kids, go to that one meeting, get the car fixed).
3. **Now, The Slash.** Look at the rest of the list. The things you feel you should do. The vacuuming. The complex dinner. The extra favor for a friend.
    - **Delete one.** Just cross it off. Decide it is not happening.
    - **Delegate one.** Ask a partner, a child, or a colleague to do it. And here is the hard part: Let them do it imperfectly. If they fold the towels wrong, let them be wrong. If they load the dishwasher inefficiently, let it go. You are buying back your sanity.
4. **Identify Your "One Thing."** What is the one thing you need for you tomorrow? Five minutes of coffee in silence? A walk around the block? Listening to a song you love? Protect that "one thing" as fiercely as you protect your work.

You are not a machine. You are a human being with limits. Honoring your limits is an act of worship.

BEDTIME PRAYER

The kitchen is closed. The work is done, or it is not, and that is okay. The lights are dimming.

It is time to take off the crown of the "Responsible One." It is heavy, and your neck needs a break.

Whisper these words to yourself. Let them be the closing ceremony of your day.

Lord of the Quiet,

I confess that I am stressed and troubled about many things. My mind is a kitchen that never closes. My heart is a list that is never checked off.

But You say my name twice. You call me out of the noise and into the silence.

Tonight, I lay down the heavy burden of holding it all together. I admit that the world will keep spinning without my help. I step over the mess, I leave the dishes, and I come to sit at Your feet.

I choose the better portion. I choose to be small. I choose to be held.

You are the Host. I am the guest. Feed my soul while I sleep.

Amen.

3

THE EXHAUSTION OF HIDING

THE STORY OF THE WOMAN AT THE WELL (JOHN 4:1-42)

The Weight of the Mask

We have talked about the exhaustion of working too hard in the story of Leah and the exhaustion of managing too much in the story of Martha. But there is a third kind of exhaustion that is quieter, darker, and perhaps the heaviest of them all.

It is the exhaustion of hiding.

It is the fatigue that comes from living a double life: not necessarily a criminal one, but a guarded one. It is the energy required to maintain the gap between who you are on the inside and who you present to the world on the outside.

We all wear masks. We have the "I'm Fine" mask we wear to church. We have the "Competent Professional" mask we wear to the office, terrified that someone will discover we are actually making it up as we go along. We have the "Patient Mother" mask we wear in public, hiding the fact that we screamed into a pillow five minutes before we left the house.

For some of you, the mask has fused to your skin. You are terrified of being truly seen.

You live with a low-grade, humming anxiety that whispers: "If they knew. If they really knew." If they knew about the credit card debt. If they knew how much you are drinking to get to sleep. If they knew the marriage is dead. If they knew you struggle with these thoughts. If they knew where you have been.

If they knew, they would leave. If they knew, the invitation would be rescinded. If they knew, the love would stop.

So, you hide. You edit your life. You curate your stories. You deflect questions with humor. You stay busy so no one has time to look you in the eye. You isolate yourself, even in a crowded room.

And my goodness, it is exhausting.

It takes a tremendous amount of effort to hold up a shield twenty-four hours a day. It drains your spirit to constantly scan the room for threats, wondering if today is the day you get exposed. You are not just tired from what you do; you are tired from who you are pretending to be.

Tonight, we are going to meet a woman who knew this exhaustion better than anyone. She was the ultimate outsider. She was a woman who walked in the heat of the day to avoid the gaze of her neighbors. She had built a fortress of shame so high she thought no one could ever scale it.

But she met a man who did not just climb the wall; He walked right through it.

THE IMMERSION

Let us go to Samaria.

The landscape is rugged, dry, and unforgiving. It is a place of history, but for the Jews of the first century, it is a place of avoidance. They walk miles out of their way to bypass this region because they believe the people here are unclean and heretical.

And in the middle of this rejected land, there is a rejected woman.

You are that woman.

It is high noon. The sun is not just a light in the sky; it is a physical weight. It beats down on the white limestone rocks, creating a shimmering haze of heat. The air is still and stifling. Even the lizards have retreated into the shade.

No one goes to the well at noon.

The well is the social center of the village. It is the ancient equivalent of the town square. The women go to the well in the cool of the morning. They go in groups. They walk arm-in-arm, their pitchers balanced on their heads, their voices weaving together in laughter and community.

But you do not go in the morning.

You wait until the sun is at its highest point, until the heat is unbearable, and until you are certain that every other woman is safely indoors. You choose the physical pain of the heat over the emotional pain of their eyes.

You know what happens when you go in the morning. The conversation stops when you approach. The whispers start behind the hands. The eyes scan you up and down, not with curiosity, but with judgment. They know your history. They know about the husbands. They know about the man you are living with now.

You are the cautionary tale of the village.

So, you walk alone.

Feel the dust on your feet. It coats your skin, settling into the cracks of your heels. Your throat is parched. The empty clay jar on your shoulder is heavy and awkward. The silence around you is deafening, broken only by the crunch of your sandals on the gravel.

You are tired of the walk. You are tired of the heat. But mostly, you are tired of the loneliness. You have built a cage of isolation to protect yourself from rejection, but the cage is lonely.

You approach Jacob's Well. You just want to get your water and get out. Get back to the shadows. Get back to hiding.

But as you round the bend, your heart drops.

There is someone there. A man.

He sits on the edge of the well, shoulders slumped with the kind of weariness you recognize in your own bones. One glance tells you He is a Jew. Your instinct is to turn around. Jews do not speak to Samaritans. And a Jewish man does not speak to a Samaritan woman alone.

So you do what you have learned to do. You keep your head down. You grip your jar tighter. You plan to move quickly. Lower the bucket. Hoist the water. Leave without eye contact.

Then He speaks.

He asks you for a drink.

You freeze. His voice is not sharp. It is not entitled. It is simply tired, human, and strangely gentle.

You look up, stunned. You are used to being ignored or judged. Being addressed like a person feels almost disorienting. You remind Him of what people like Him do not do. You name the boundary out loud, Jew and Samaritan, man and woman, stranger and outcast. You are telling Him, "This is not how this works."

But He does not retreat behind the rules. He looks at you as if the rules are not the most important thing about you. He speaks about God's gift, and about who it is that is asking you. He turns your attention from the well at your feet to a deeper thirst you have carried for years. He offers something He calls "living water."

Living water.

For a moment, you forget the heat and the shame and the careful way you have learned to hold yourself. For a moment, you are simply having a conversation. And it feels like air in your lungs.

Then the conversation shifts.

He stops speaking in images and goes straight to the center of your life. He tells you to go get your husband and come back.

The blood drains from your face. The day suddenly feels colder. Panic rises in your throat. This is the moment when your past catches up to you. If you tell the truth, the whole story, the failures, the losses, the way you have been discarded and used, you expect Him to recoil.

So you reach for your mask. You give Him the safest sentence you can manage. You tell Him you do not have a husband.

You hold your breath, hoping He will move on.

He does not.

He stays with you, and with a gentleness that almost hurts, He tells you He already knows. He names the husbands. He names the number. He names the truth about the man you are with now.

The jar slips on your shoulder. The world tilts.

He knows the history. He knows the heartbreak. He knows what you have tried to bury. It is as if He has read your whole life and laid it open in the sunlight.

You stand there exposed. The mask is gone. The walls are down. There is nowhere left to hide. You wait for rejection. You wait for Him to stand up and walk away from the unclean woman.

But He stays.

He does not flinch. He does not look away.

And in that moment, the exhaustion breaks.

THE CONNECTION

Let us sit down on the edge of the well together.

We do not carry clay jars anymore, but the dynamic is exactly the same. We are terrified of being fully known.

You might not have five ex-husbands. Your shame might look very different. Maybe it is the credit card debt your family does not know about. Maybe it is the eating disorder you thought you beat that has crept back in. Maybe it is the way you yell at your kids. Maybe it is just the overwhelming sense that you are a fraud: that if people saw the mess inside your head, they would realize you are not the "good Christian woman" you pretend to be.

This is the exhaustion of imposter syndrome.

It is the belief that love is contingent on your performance of goodness. You believe that you are only lovable as long as you are keeping it together.

So you hide.

You avoid deep community because deep community requires vulnerability. You keep your prayers surface-level because you are afraid to admit the truth to God. You tell the half-truth: "I'm good! Just busy!"

You do this to stay safe. But hiding is lonely work. Shame is the fear of disconnection. It is the thought: "Is there something about me that, if people see it, I will not be worthy of connection?"

The tragedy is that this hiding keeps us from the very thing we are starving for. We want to be loved, but we can only be loved if we are known. If you hide who you are, and people love the mask, you will never feel truly loved because they are loving a fake.

You are tired because you are guarding a fortress that God wants to tear down.

THE RELEASE

Let us go back to the moment of exposure at the well.

Jesus brought her hidden life into the light. He named what she had been trying to keep buried. And then He stayed.

He did not uncover her story to humiliate her. He uncovered it to heal her. He showed her that He knew the thing she feared most, and He was still speaking to her with dignity. Still asking for a drink. Still offering her something that could finally satisfy the thirst beneath all her other thirsts.

This is grace. Grace is not God loving you because you are good. Grace is God knowing the truth about you and loving you anyway.

Notice the order of it. Jesus spoke to her before the subject of her husbands ever surfaced. He treated her like a person before she explained herself. He met her in the mess, not after she cleaned it up.

Then something beautiful happens. The woman leaves her water jar and goes back into the city.

She leaves the jar.

She came to the well carrying weight, the physical weight of the task and the spiritual weight of shame. But after meeting the Messiah, after being seen and known, she is so unburdened that she forgets the very errand she came for. She leaves the jar behind in the dust.

And she runs back to the village, back to the very people she had been avoiding. She calls them to come and see. She points them to the One who knew her whole story.

Look at the transformation. Minutes ago, she was hiding from those people. Now she is speaking openly, even about the parts of her life she once tried to conceal. The thing she feared would ruin her becomes the very thing God uses to draw others. Her secret becomes her testimony.

The exhaustion of hiding begins to evaporate the moment she realizes she has nothing left to hide.

The release for you tonight is this. You are already known.

God already sees. He was there. He heard the thought. You are not keeping secrets from Him. You are only keeping yourself from the relief of being honest.

His love is not fragile. It does not shatter when it touches the truth of who you are. He is not waiting for the future version of you who has everything fixed. He is waiting for you. The you at noon. The you with the messy history.

He sees you. He knows you. And He loves you.

THE INVITATION

You might be thinking: "I can't just run into my town and tell everyone my secrets."

And you do not have to. Vulnerability requires safety. But you do need to practice being naked before God.

We are going to do a simple breath prayer. This is an ancient practice that connects the rhythm of your body with the truth of the Spirit. It physically calms your nervous system while anchoring your mind.

The "Unmasking" Breath Prayer

1. **Find a quiet space.** Lie in bed or sit in a comfortable chair. Close your eyes.

2. **The Inhale (The Truth).** Take a slow, deep breath in through your nose for a count of four. As you inhale, think these words: "You know everything about me."

3. **The Exhale (The Grace).** Release the breath slowly through your mouth for a count of six. As you exhale, think these words: "And You love me still."

4. **Repeat.** Do this ten times. Feel the relief of being known and loved. Notice how your shoulders drop. You do not have to pretend here.

BEDTIME PRAYER

The sun has set on Samaria. The jar is left behind. The mask is on the floor. It is just you and God now.

Whisper these words into the safety of the dark.

God of the noon day sun, God of the shadows, God who meets me at the well,

I am tired of hiding. I am tired of carrying the heavy jar of my reputation. I am tired of editing my soul, trimming the truth down to something safer, something more acceptable.

Tonight, I confess what is already true. You know me. You know the number of hairs on my head and the number of mistakes in my heart. You have read my entire story, every chapter I wish I could rewrite, and You did not close the book.

So I step out of the shadows. I loosen my grip on the image I have tried to protect. I stop managing what people think and bring You what I actually am. Meet me here with mercy. Wash what is stained. Heal what is bruised. Quiet the shame that keeps trying to name me.

I receive the living water I did not earn. Let it sink deeper than my fear, deeper than my history, deeper than the labels I have carried. Fill the places that have been dry for so long.

I am fully known. I am fully loved. And by Your grace, I am finally free.

Amen.

PART II

THE EXHAUSTION
OF DEPLETION

Stories for when you have nothing left to give.

We move now from the exhaustion of striving, which is working to prove your worth, to the exhaustion of depletion, which is simply running out of resources.

This section is for the woman who has scraped the bottom of the barrel. It is for the woman who looks at her bank account, her emotional reserves, or her physical energy and sees a zero balance. It is for the woman who feels like she is surviving, not living.

In the desert of depletion, we do not need a lecture on how to manage our resources better. We need a miracle. Tonight, we meet a woman who found one in the most unlikely place.

4

THE EXHAUSTION OF SURVIVAL

THE STORY OF THE WIDOW OF ZAREPHATH (1 KINGS 17:8-16)

The Math of Scarcity

There is a specific kind of exhaustion that comes from math.

It is not the math of schoolbooks or spreadsheets, but the frantic, high-stakes mental math of survival. If I pay the electric bill today, can I still buy groceries on Friday? If I give this much energy to my job, will I have anything left for my children when I get home? If I say yes to this crisis, will I collapse?

It is the math of subtraction. It is the relentless calculation of checking your reserves and realizing that the demands on your life are greater than the supply.

This is the exhaustion of survival.

It is a primal, gnawing fatigue. It settles in the pit of your stomach. It keeps you up at night with a racing heart, panic tightening your throat, as you wonder how you are going to make it through the month, the week, or even just the next hour.

When you are in survival mode, your world shrinks. You stop dreaming about the future because you are too busy trying to secure the present. You stop looking at the horizon and start looking at your feet, just trying to take one more step without falling. You become hyper-focused on what you lack.

You see the empty chair. You see the empty bank account. You see the empty eyes of the people relying on you.

Perhaps the most terrifying part of this exhaustion is the feeling of inevitability. You feel like you are sliding down a slow slope toward a cliff, and you have run out of branches to grab. You are tired of fighting gravity. You are ready to let go.

If you are holding your breath right now, if your shoulders are up by your ears, or if you feel like you are clinging to the edge by your fingernails, this story is for you.

We are going to travel to a place called Zarephath. We are going to meet a woman who had done the math, and the answer was zero. She was preparing for the end, but she was about to meet the God of new beginnings.

THE IMMERSION

The silence of the house is the loudest thing in the world.

You are a widow living in Zarephath, a coastal town in Sidon. It is a time of drought. This is not just a dry spell, but a catastrophic, earth-cracking famine that has lasted for years. The sky is like bronze: hard, unyielding, and cloudless. The ground is like iron.

You have watched the world slowly die around you. First, the crops withered in the fields. Then the livestock thinned and disappeared. Then the neighbors stopped talking, saving their breath and their energy. Now, the silence of death hangs over the entire village.

You are alone. Your husband is gone, leaving you with no protector in a society that ignores women without men. You have a son, a small boy with eyes that seem too big for his thinning face.

Every day for months, you have played the game of rationing. You take less for yourself so there is a little more for him. You provide just one cake today and just half a cake tomorrow. You water down the oil and scrape the sides of the jar.

You have been the magician of your home, stretching resources that should have run out weeks ago. You have prayed to every god you know. You have bartered everything of value you own.

But today, the magic has run out.

You walk into your kitchen, which is a dark, cool corner of your small home. You lift the lid of the flour jar. It is a sound you will never forget: the hollow, scratchy sound of ceramic against ceramic as you scrape the ladle across the bottom. Scrape. Scrape. Dust. That is all that is left. A handful of white dust.

You tip the jug of oil. A few thick drops slide out, sluggish and final.

You do the math. A handful of flour and a few drops of oil. It is enough for one small loaf of bread. One tiny, flat cake. And then? Nothing. There is no money to buy more. There is no neighbor to borrow from because they are starving, too. There is no rain on the horizon.

This is it. The end of the line.

A strange calm settles over you. It is the calm of resignation. You are done fighting. You are done hoping. Hope is too expensive; it costs energy you do not have.

You look at your son sleeping in the corner. You decide not to wake him yet. You will go out, gather some wood, cook this last meal, and then you will hold him while you both wait for death. It is a grim plan, but it is a plan. It is better than the uncertainty.

You step out into the blinding sunlight. The heat hits you like a phys-ical blow. You walk toward the city gate, your eyes scanning the dust for sticks. Even the wood is scarce.

You bend down to pick up a twig. Your head swims with hunger. You stumble, catch yourself, and straighten up.

And then you see him.

A man is sitting near the gate. He looks as rough as the land itself: hair wild, cloak dusty, and eyes burning with a strange intensity. He is a foreigner, an Israelite.

He speaks to you: "Please, bring me a little water in a cup so that I may drink."

You hesitate. Water is precious. But hospitality is a reflex, deeply ingrained. Perhaps, in your final hours, you want to offer one last act of kindness. You turn to go get the water.

But then his voice stops you again.

"And please, bring me a piece of bread as well."

The request hits you like a slap. Bread? Does he not see the ribs showing through your tunic? Does he not know that the entire land is starving? How dare he ask for bread?

The resignation breaks, and a flash of raw honesty pours out of you. You turn to him and you swear by his God, acknowledging his faith even in your despair.

"As surely as the Lord your God lives, I don't have any bread. I only have a handful of flour in a jar and a little olive oil in a jug. I am gath-ering a few sticks to take home and make a final meal for myself and my son, so that we may eat it and die."

There it is. You said it. You spoke the unspeakable: "eat it, and die." You laid your poverty bare before this stranger. You expect him to apologize. You expect him to say, "I am so sorry, I did not know." You expect him to withdraw his request and let you go to your funeral meal in peace.

But he does not.

Elijah looks at you. He sees the terror in your eyes. He sees the shadow of death hovering over your son. And he says the most audacious, impossible thing.

"Don't be afraid. Go home and do as you said. But first, make a small loaf of bread for me from what you have and bring it to me, and then make something for yourself and your son. For this is what the Lord, the God of Israel, says: 'The jar of flour will not be used up and the jug of oil will not run dry until the day the Lord sends rain on the land.'"

Feed him first.

The sheer insanity of the request makes your head spin. You have just told him you have enough for one meal, a final meal for a dying child. And he is asking you to give it to him? He is asking you to take the last crumb of sustenance out of the mouth of your son and give it to a stranger?

It feels cruel. It feels impossible. It violates every instinct of a mother.

But he gave you a promise that defies the laws of nature.

You stand there in the dust, holding your two sticks. You have a choice. You can cling to your scarcity. You can hoard that last handful of flour, eat it, and accept the end. That is the logical choice. That is the safe choice. Or, you can risk everything. You can open your hand. You can give away the only thing you have left, trusting in a word from a God you do not even know.

It is the hardest thing you have ever done.

You walk back to your kitchen. You light the fire with the two sticks. You take the jar. You pour out the flour. All of it. You mix it with the oil. You knead the dough.

You bake the bread. The smell fills the house: the smell of life in a place of death.

You take the warm loaf. You walk out to the stranger. You hand it to him. Your hands are empty now. You have nothing left.

You walk back inside, preparing to explain to your son why there is no food. You look at the jar on the table. The jar you just emptied.

And you see something white at the bottom.

You blink. You step closer. You reach in. Flour. A handful. Just enough for one more loaf.

You grab the oil jug. You tip it. Oil flows. Just enough.

You bake another loaf. You and your son eat. Your bellies are full for the first time in months. You sleep.

The next morning, you wake up. The fear rushes back instantly. Was it a dream? You run to the kitchen. You lift the lid. Empty? No. A handful. Just enough.

And the next day. And the next. For days, weeks, months, or maybe years, the miracle repeats. The jar never overflows. It is never full to the brim. You never open a warehouse of grain. But every single morning, when you scrape the bottom, there is always, always just enough for today.

THE CONNECTION

Let us leave the ancient kitchen and sit at your kitchen table.

You might not be measuring flour for a final meal, but I know you understand the exhaustion of survival.

I know what it is like to look at your bank account and realize the numbers do not add up. I know the feeling of financial anxiety: robbing Peter to pay Paul, shuffling bills, juggling due dates, and living in the constant, low-level nausea of insecurity.

But this exhaustion is not always only about money. Sometimes it is about emotional scarcity.

It is the feeling when your child is crying for attention, your spouse needs support, your boss needs another project, and your friend needs a shoulder to cry on, and you look inside your emotional jar, and it is empty. You have scraped the bottom. You have nothing left to give. You want to scream: "I am gathering two sticks to go die! Leave me alone!"

You are operating in a deficit. You are giving out more than you are taking in. Like the widow, you have resigned yourself to the idea that this is just how it is. This is your lot. You will always be tired. You will always be running on fumes.

Into this depletion, God comes with a request that feels offensive: "Give me what you have. Trust me with the last bit."

It feels counterintuitive. When we are scared, our instinct is to hoard. We grip tighter. We close our hands. We protect the little we have left because we are terrified that if we let go, we will die.

We think that security looks like a full warehouse. We think peace looks like a million dollars in the bank, or a perfect marriage, or a life with no problems. We think: "God, if You give me an overflow, then I will trust You."

But the story of the widow of Zarephath teaches us a hard, beautiful truth: God is rarely the God of the warehouse. He is the God of the daily bread.

THE RELEASE

The miracle in Zarephath was not a lottery win.

Please catch this distinction. God did not fill her house with sacks of grain. He did not make her rich. If you looked at her jar at any given moment in the afternoon, it probably looked empty.

She had to wake up every single morning and trust that the flour would be there. She had to live in a state of constant dependence.

For us, the responsible women, this sounds terrifying. We hate dependence. We want control. We want to see the five-year plan. We want the security of abundance so we do not have to bother God with our needs.

But God knows that independence is often just a fancy word for distance. If He gave us the warehouse, we would stop talking to Him. We would rely on our storage instead of our Savior.

So, He keeps us in the rhythm of the jar. Scrape. Trust. Eat. Repeat.

The release for you tonight is the realization that "just enough" is a miracle.

If you made it through today, that is a miracle. If you had enough patience for your toddler just for today, that is the provision of God. If the money covered the bills just for this month, that is the oil flowing.

You are exhausting yourself trying to secure the future. You are worrying about flour for next year, for when the kids go to college, or for when you retire. You are grieving the emptiness of a jar you have not even opened yet.

God is asking you to stop living in the imaginary future of scarcity and live in the present reality of His provision.

He is saying: "I am not giving you grace for next year yet. I am giving you grace for this breath. And when you take the next breath, I will be there, too."

The widow did not die. Her son did not die. They lived, day by day, on the faithfulness of God. And so will you.

You are not going to run dry. You are not going to be abandoned. The bottom of the jar is not the end of the story; it is the place where God shows up.

THE INVITATION

We carry our stress in our hands. Have you noticed? When we are anxious about money or the future, we literally clench our fists. We hold on tight, as if our grip is the only thing keeping the world from spinning off its axis.

Tonight, we are going to practice the physical act of release.

The "Open Hands" Gesture

1. **Sit comfortably.** If you are in bed, lie on your back. If you are in a chair, place your feet on the floor.
2. **The Clench.** First, I want you to acknowledge the fear. Clench your hands into fists. Squeeze them tight. Feel the tension in your knuckles, your wrists, and your forearms. Think about the scarcity. The bills. The energy drain. The fear of the future. Hold it all in those fists. Hold it tight. Notice how tiring it is to hold on.
3. **The Release.** Now, on a count of three, I want you to exhale and pop your hands open. One... Two... Three... OPEN.
4. **The Posture.** Let your hands lie open, palms facing up, fingers curled naturally and loosely. This is the posture of receiving. You cannot receive fresh bread if your hands are clenched around old fears.
5. **The Declaration.** In your mind, say: "My hands are open. I am not the source. You are the source." Keep your hands open for a minute. Feel the blood flow back into your fingers. Feel the surrender.

BEDTIME PRAYER

The fire is out. The last cake has been eaten. The jar looks empty again. But we know the secret now. We know that the emptiness is just the canvas for the miracle of tomorrow.

Whisper these words into the dark.

God of the empty jar, God of the widow, God of the wilderness,

I confess that I am scared of the bottom. I am scared of running out. I have been checking the math, and it does not add up.

But You are not a God of math. You are a God of multiplication.

I have scraped the bottom of my strength today. I have nothing left to give. So I bring You my emptiness.

I trust You for the bread of tomorrow. I trust You for the patience of tomorrow. I trust You for the hope of tomorrow.

The jar will not run dry. The oil will not fail. You are enough. You are enough. You are enough.

Amen.

5

THE EXHAUSTION OF CHRONIC PAIN

THE STORY OF THE BLEEDING WOMAN (MARK 5:25-34)

T he Body Betrayed

We have spoken about the exhaustion of the mind, the racing thoughts, and the exhaustion of the spirit, the striving for worth. But there is an exhaustion that lives closer to home. It lives in your very cells. It lives in your joints, your nerves, and your blood.

This is the exhaustion of chronic pain.

It is a lonely, peculiar kind of tiredness. It is the exhaustion of waking up after eight hours of sleep and feeling like you have run a marathon in the night. It is the exhaustion of having to calculate your energy like a limited currency: knowing that if you take a shower, you might not have the strength to cook dinner. If you go to the grocery store, you might need two days to recover.

For many of you reading this, your body has become an unsafe place.

You are living with autoimmune flare-ups that strike without warning. You are navigating the fog of fibromyalgia, the stabbing lights of migraines, the silent battles of endometriosis, or the crushing weight of depression that manifests as physical lead in your limbs.

And perhaps the hardest part is the invisibility of it. You look "fine." You put on makeup. You smile at church. You show up to work. And because you do not have a cast on your leg or a bandage on your head, the world assumes you are well. They ask, "Why are you so tired?" They say, "You just need to exercise more," or "Have you tried kale?" or "Maybe it is stress."

They do not see the war you are fighting inside your own skin.

They do not know that being "sick and tired" is not just a figure of speech for you; it is a diagnosis. It is a state of being.

You grieve the woman you used to be: the one who could spend an hour at the gym, who could stay up late talking with friends, and who did not have to carry a pharmacy in her purse. You feel betrayed by your own vessel. You feel trapped.

And sometimes, in the dark, you wonder where God is in the pain. Does He care about biology? Or is He only interested in your soul? Does He see the bruises? Does He feel the ache?

Tonight, we are going to meet a woman who spent 4,380 days in pain. She was anonymous, broke, and isolated. She was the definition of "chronic." And she is going to show us what happens when we bring our broken bodies to the feet of God.

THE IMMERSION

Let us go to the seaside town of Capernaum.

The air is salty and thick. The streets are narrow, crowded with fishermen, merchants, and children. But you are not part of the bustle. You are hugging the walls, keeping your head covered, and trying to shrink into the stone.

You are the woman with the "issue of blood."

The Bible does not give you a name. It defines you by your sickness. For twelve years, a lifetime in that era, you have been bleeding.

Imagine the physical reality of that. Twelve years of constant hemorrhage. Twelve years of anemia. Your skin is pale, almost translucent. Your hands shake with a permanent tremor of weakness. You are always cold, even in the heat of summer, because your blood is too thin to hold warmth. You are dizzy when you stand up too fast. You are breathless just walking across the room.

But the physical pain is only half the torture. The other half is the isolation.

According to the Levitical law of your time, your condition makes you unclean. Anything you touch becomes unclean. Anyone who touches you becomes unclean. You cannot sit on a communal bench. You cannot hug your friends. You cannot prepare food for your family. You cannot enter the synagogue to pray. You cannot sleep in the same bed as your husband, if he has not already divorced you.

You are a ghost in your own life. You watch the world from a distance, weddings, festivals, and Sabbath dinners, unable to participate. You are untouchable. To touch another human being is to contaminate them.

And then, there are the doctors.

Scripture gives us a heartbreaking summary of your medical story. For years, you sought help from physician after physician, spending everything you had, only to find no relief. In fact, you grew worse.

Think about that. You did not only suffer from the disease. You suffered through the treatments.

For twelve long years, you chased every rumor of hope. You traveled to specialists. You swallowed bitter herbs. You endured painful procedures. You paid for costly ointments. You even tried the superstitious "cures" whispered by village healers, the kind that promised much and delivered nothing. You tried it all.

And every time, you paid. You reached into your savings until the bag was empty. You sold your jewelry. You sold your furniture. You are destitute now.

And for what? You grew worse.

The despair is a physical weight. You are twelve years older, twelve years weaker, and penniless. You have scraped the bottom of the jar of hope, and there is nothing left.

But today, there is a noise in the street.

A rumor is moving through the town like wildfire. Jesus of Nazareth is here. The Rabbi who heals lepers. The Rabbi who makes the blind see. He is passing through.

A spark flares in the ashes of your heart, desperate and dangerous in its hope. You tell yourself that if you can only reach out and touch the edge of His garment, you will be made well.

You do not need a conversation. You do not need Him to lay hands on you; you would not dare ask, as you are unclean. You just need contact. A brush of the hem. A stolen miracle.

You step out into the street. It is a nightmare. A massive crowd is pressing around Jesus.

It is a wall of bodies: shoulders, elbows, and backs. For a healthy person, it is difficult navigation. For a frail, anemic woman, it is a fortress.

If they recognize you, they will shout at you. They will stone you for being unclean in a crowd. You have to be invisible.

So, you drop down.

You get on your hands and knees. You crawl into the forest of legs. Imagine the dust choking you. Imagine the smell of hundreds of unwashed feet. Imagine the terrifying risk of being trampled. Sandals stomp inches from your fingers. Knees knock against your ribs. You are kicked, shoved, and jostled. You are breathing hard, your heart hammering against your thin chest like a trapped bird. You are weak, so weak. Every inch is a battle.

But then you see Him. Through the gaps in the crowd, you catch sight of His feet. And there, brushing the dust, hang the blue and white tassels at the corners of His garment.

Just one more foot. Just a little closer. You stretch out your arm. Your fingers are trembling. You reach through the legs of a fisherman. You reach past the guard of a disciple. You brush your fingertips against the rough wool of the tassel.

Zap.

It is not a sound; it is a sensation. Instantly, in the time it takes to blink, the flow of blood stops. You feel it. You know your own body better than any doctor. You feel the seal. You feel the warmth rushing back into your cold limbs. You feel a surge of strength that you have not felt in a decade. The pain is gone. The cramping is gone. The sickness is gone. It worked.

You pull your hand back, clutching it to your chest, tears springing to your eyes. I did it. I am free. You start to scramble backward, preparing to disappear into the crowd, to take your miracle and run home to start your new life.

But the movement stops. The feet stop. The crowd stops.

A voice cuts through the noise: "Who touched my clothes?"

Your heart stutters to a stop. No. Please, no.

The disciples look around at the packed crowd and confusion. Everyone is pushing in. Everyone is brushing past Him. How could anyone possibly identify one touch among so many?

But He does not let it go. He stops and searches, certain that something has just changed. He knows power has gone out from Him, and

He will not move on until the one who reached for Him is brought into the open.

He is looking around. His eyes are scanning the crowd. He is looking for you. He felt it. He felt the drain. He felt the transaction.

You have a choice. You can run. You can stay hidden in the dirt. But something about His voice, something about the way He halted the entire universe just to find the source of the touch, makes you stay.

Trembling with fear, you stand up. You are covered in dust. You are shaking. The crowd parts. Everyone is looking at you now. The exposure you feared for twelve years has happened.

You fall at His feet. And you tell Him the truth. The whole truth. The twelve years. The suffering. The doctors. The poverty. The shame. The touch. The healing. You pour it all out in front of everyone.

You wait for the rebuke. You wait for Him to be angry that an unclean woman contaminated a holy Rabbi. You wait for Him to take the healing back.

He looks at you. He looks at your tired face, your dusty hands, and your trembling frame. And He says the one word that changes everything.

"Daughter."

Not "Woman." Not "Sinner." Not "Unclean One." "Daughter."

It is the only time in the Gospels Jesus directly addresses a woman this way. He calls her daughter not to diminish her, but to name her as belonging. Then He affirms her faith, sends her away in peace, and tells her she is healed of her affliction.

THE CONNECTION

Let us sit in the quiet of your room for a moment.

I know that for many of you, the story has not ended with the "Zap" yet. You have touched the hem, you have prayed the prayers, and you have seen the doctors, but the pain is still there. The blood has not stopped. The fatigue has not lifted.

And that is a specific, crushing kind of grief.

You know the exhaustion of the waiting room. You know the cycle of hope and disappointment. You hear about a new specialist, a new diet, or a new supplement. You get your hopes up. You spend the money. You try the protocol. And three months later, you are back where you started, only poorer and more discouraged.

You know the exhaustion of advocacy. You have to be your own doctor because no one else seems to put the puzzle pieces together. You have to bring binders of medical records to appointments. You have to fight insurance companies. You have to convince people that your pain is real.

And worst of all, you know the exhaustion of guilt. You feel guilty for being the "sick friend." You feel guilty that your husband has to pick up the slack. You feel guilty that you cannot play on the floor with your kids. You feel like a burden.

And sometimes, deep down, you wonder if God is punishing you. You wonder: "If I had more faith, would I be well?"

Let me stop you right there. That is a lie from the pit. The bleeding woman did not have perfect theology. She was superstitious! She thought touching a piece of cloth would work like magic. She did not ask permission. She did not pray a perfect prayer. She just reached out in desperation. And Jesus honored it.

Her healing was not a reward for her good behavior; it was a response to her need.

But here is the connection I want you to see tonight: Jesus stopped.

He was on His way to heal a dying twelve-year-old girl. It was a Code Blue emergency. Time was critical. And yet, He stopped the procession. He stopped the urgency. He stopped the important people. Why? To look at a woman with a chronic illness.

This tells me everything I need to know about how God views your pain. He does not view your body as an inconvenience. He does not view your chronic condition as a distraction from His real work. You are the work.

He felt the power go out of Him. Think about that. The God of the universe is attuned to your physical body. He feels the drain. He feels the cost. He is not indifferent to your biology.

When you are lying in bed, staring at the ceiling, wondering if anyone understands the ache in your bones, know this: Jesus stopped for it.

THE RELEASE

There is a profound release in the word "Daughter."

For twelve years, this woman was defined by what she was not. She was not clean. She was not healthy. She was not welcome. She was not worthy.

In one word, Jesus gave her a new identity: she was restored to the family. He did not just heal her body; He healed her status. He made sure that everyone in that crowd knew she was no longer an outcast. She was a Daughter of the King.

But there is another release here, specifically for those with chronic pain. It is the release of validation.

Jesus tells her that her faith has made her well. The Greek verb used there is *sōzō*, a word that can mean more than physical healing. It carries the sense of being restored and made whole, in body, soul, and spirit.

Then He sends her away in peace. That word echoes the Hebrew idea of *shalom*, which is not merely the absence of trouble. It is deep well-being. It is flourishing. It is wholeness. It is life put back into its right order.

The release for you tonight is to know that God cares about your body.

We often have a Gnostic view of Christianity: we think the body is just a wrapper, a shell, or a rental car for the soul. We think God only cares about our heart. But the Incarnation proves us wrong. God became flesh. He had feet that got dusty. He had a stomach that growled. He had nerves that felt pain.

He honors your body, even in its brokenness.

Maybe your healing has not come yet. Maybe you are still in the twelve years. I cannot promise you that touching the hem will fix your autoimmune disease tonight. I wish I could. But I can promise you this: you do not have to clean up your body to meet Jesus.

You do not have to be well to be close to Him. You do not have to have energy to be used by Him. You do not have to hide the messy, bleeding, aching parts of yourself.

He meets you in the dust. He meets you on the floor. He meets you in the flare-up. And He does not recoil. He does not step back to avoid contamination. He leans in. He calls you "Daughter."

He says, "I know you are tired. I know it hurts. I am not angry at your weakness. I am right here in it with you."

Your pain is not a sign of His absence; it is the place where His presence draws nearest.

THE INVITATION

When we live with chronic pain, it is easy to treat our bodies like enemies. We ignore them, numb them, or resent them. We retreat into our heads because our bodies feel like a torture chamber.

Tonight, I want to invite you to do something difficult. I want you to befriend your body again. Not the body you wish you had, but the body you have.

We are going to do a Body Scan of Gratitude.

This is not about pretending the pain is not there. It is about acknowledging that your body is fighting for you, not against you. It is doing the best it can under impossible circumstances.

The "Body Scan" Relaxation

1. **Get Comfortable.** Lie down on your bed. Support your neck and knees with pillows if needed. Close your eyes.
2. **The Feet.** Bring your attention to your toes and feet. Wiggle them gently. Think: "Thank you, feet. You carried me today. Even when I was tired, you held me up." Release: Let your feet grow heavy and soft.
3. **The Legs and Hips.** Move your attention to your calves, knees, and hips. Notice any tension or ache. Do not judge it. Just notice it. Think: "Thank you, legs. You allowed me to stand. Thank you, hips, for carrying the weight." Release: Let your legs sink into the mattress.
4. **The Belly and Chest.** Focus on your stomach and your lungs. Feel the rise and fall. Think: "Thank you, organs, for digesting, for beating, for breathing without me even asking. You are working so hard to keep me alive." Release: Unclench your stomach. Let your breath deepen.
5. **The Hands and Arms.** Notice your fingers and shoulders. Think: "Thank you, hands. You held the cup. You typed the words. You stroked the child's hair. You did good work today." Release: Drop your shoulders away from your ears. Open your palms.

6. **The Head and Face.** Notice your jaw, your eyes, and your forehead. Think: "Thank you, brain. You navigated the fog. You kept me safe." Release: Soften your jaw. Smooth your brow.

7. **The Whole Body.** Say: "Dear Body, I am sorry I have hated you. I know you are doing your best. We are on the same team. I accept you. I thank you. You can rest now."

BEDTIME PRAYER

The doctors' offices are closed. The Google searches are done for the night. The medication has been taken. Now, we commit this vessel to its Maker.

Whisper these words to the One who knit you together.

God of the Flesh and Bone, God of the Hem, God who stops for me,

I bring You my tired body tonight. I bring You the aches, the weakness, and the frustration. I bring You the years of disappointment.

Thank You that You do not demand I be well to be loved. Thank You that my pain does not make me unclean in Your sight. Thank You that You feel the power go out; You know the cost.

I touch the hem of Your garment now. If You choose to heal, I will receive it with joy. If You choose to hold, I will receive it with trust.

I am not just a patient. I am not just a diagnosis. I am Your Daughter. And that is enough.

Go in peace, my soul. Go in peace, my body.

Amen.

6

THE EXHAUSTION OF BEING INVISIBLE

THE STORY OF HAGAR
(GENESIS 16:1-16; 21:8-21)

T he Ghost in the Machine

We have arrived at a kind of exhaustion that is difficult to describe because, by its very nature, it goes unnoticed.

It is not the loud exhaustion of the CEO running a company. It is not the public exhaustion of the marathon runner. It is the quiet, dissolving exhaustion of the person who keeps the world running from the shadows.

This is the exhaustion of being invisible.

It is the specific fatigue of being treated as a function rather than a person. It is the feeling of being a utility, like a light switch or a faucet. People expect you to work when they need you, and they ignore you when they do not.

I am speaking to the mother who feels like a glorified housekeeper. You pick up the socks, you wash the dishes, you drive the carpool, you make the appointments. Your family moves around you, eating the food you cooked and wearing the clothes you washed, but no one looks you in the eye. You wonder: "If I disappeared tomorrow, would they miss me? Or would they just miss the laundry getting done?"

I am speaking to the employee who does the heavy lifting on the project, only to watch the boss take the credit in the meeting. You are the background character in your own career. You are the one staying late to fix the formatting while others go out for drinks. You feel used. You feel discarded.

I am speaking to the friend who is always the listener, never the listened to. You are the emotional dumping ground for everyone else's crisis, but when you try to speak about your own pain, the room goes silent or the subject changes.

This exhaustion is heavy because it comes with a deep, corrosive sense of worthlessness. You start to believe the lie: "I only matter as long as I am useful." You start to feel like a ghost in your own life: present, but unseen, passing through rooms without leaving a ripple.

Tonight, we are going to look at a woman who was the ultimate utility in Scripture. She was a slave. She was a surrogate. She was a disposable piece of property in the tent of a wealthy man.

Her name was Hagar. She is the only person in Scripture who is explicitly described as giving God a name. Think about that. Not a king. Not a prophet. A runaway, pregnant Egyptian slave girl. And the name she gives Him changes everything for those of us who feel invisible.

THE IMMERSION

Let us step into the heat of the Negev Desert.

Before we get to the desert, we must start in the tent of Abram and Sarai. To the world, this is a tent of promise. This is the home of the patriarch and matriarch of the faith. But to you, Hagar, it is a house of servitude.

You are Egyptian. You likely entered this household as property, part of an exchange you never controlled. You have no status here. No protection. No voice. You are useful for what you can carry, clean, and fetch.

And then one day, you become useful in a different way.

Sarai cannot conceive, and in her grief she decides to build a future through you. You are not treated like a person with agency. You are treated like a solution. Scripture does not show anyone asking what you want. You are given to Abram to bear a child, not out of love, but out of necessity.

When you become pregnant, you might expect things to improve. You are carrying Abram's child. Surely that means you will be seen now. Surely that means you will matter.

Instead, the atmosphere in the tent turns toxic.

Sarai's jealousy sharpens into mistreatment. What begins as tension becomes harsh affliction. And Abram does not intervene. He steps back and leaves you under Sarai's authority, as if what is happening to you is not his responsibility.

You are no longer a help. You are a complication.

So you run.

You are pregnant. You are young. You have no supplies, no plan, and no protector. But the wilderness feels safer than that tent.

You head toward Egypt, into the desert of Shur. The sun bears down like a weight. The sand scorches your feet. Your throat goes dry. You are carrying two lives, and both feel fragile.

Finally, you collapse by a spring of water. Alone. Unprotected. An escaped slave in a world that sees you as lost property. In the eyes of everyone else, you are easy to discard.

But God does not discard you.

He meets you there. He speaks your name. Not a label. Not a role. Your name. He sees where you have come from, and He sees where you are headed, even when you cannot imagine a future beyond the next hour.

And the story does not end at that spring.

You return. The baby is born. Ishmael grows. For years you survive in the same household that broke you.

Then Sarah has her own son, Isaac. And once again, you become the problem. This time Abraham sends you away for good, with a little food and a skin of water. You walk into the wilderness of Beersheba with your son and almost nothing else.

The water runs out. The skin goes empty. Ishmael, now older but weak with thirst, collapses. You cannot carry him. You cannot bear to watch him die.

So you place him under a bush and walk away far enough that you do not have to see the end up close. You sit in the dust and break open with grief. Not polite tears, but the kind of sobbing that comes from the deepest place in the soul. The grief of a woman who has been used and dismissed, as if her life only mattered when it bene-fited someone else.

The heat shimmers on the horizon. The wind moves through the scrub. The chosen family is back in their tent, and you are out here disappearing.

And then you hear a voice.

Not the voice of a master. Not the voice of a mistress. A voice that comes with authority and mercy.

He calls you by name again.

God does not let you die unknown in the desert. He comes to you by the spring, and He comes to you by the bush. He hears the cries no one else hears. He sees the woman the world overlooks, and He makes it clear that your story is not finished.

THE CONNECTION

Let us leave the desert wind and step into the fluorescent lights of your office, or the quiet chaos of your living room.

You might not be a runaway slave, but you know the ache of Hagar.

This chapter is for the default parent. You are the one who remembers that it is Wacky Hair Day at school. You are the one who notices that the toddler has a rash before anyone else does. You are the one who researches the best car seat, the best vitamins, and the best summer camp. You are also the one who keeps track of the teenager's crazy schedule, the last minute rides, the missing hoodie that has somehow become an emergency, and the project that is due tomorrow but somehow only surfaced tonight. When things go smoothly, no one says anything. But when things go wrong? When the jersey is not washed? When the permission slip is lost? When the teen shows up late and needs someone to blame? The eyes turn to you. You feel like a servant in your own home. You feel that your value is tied to your output. You wonder if anyone sees you, if anyone asks how you are doing, or if they only care that the machine keeps running.

This chapter is for the office workhorse. You are the reliable one, the one who cleans up the messes left by the charismatic visionaries. You are the one staying late to make sure the presentation actually works. Yet, when the promotions are handed out, you are overlooked. You are told you are "too valuable in your current role" to be moved. Translation: You are too useful as a servant to be treated as a queen. You feel used. You feel like a tool that is put back in the drawer until it is needed again.

This chapter is for the discarded friend. You were the one they called when they were going through a breakup. You picked up the phone even when it was late at night. You listened for hours. But now that they are dating someone new? Now that they are happy? Silence. You were a placeholder, a bridge to get them from one season to the next. Now that they have crossed over, they do not need the bridge anymore.

The exhaustion of invisibility is dangerous because it makes us want to disappear completely. We think: "Fine. If I do not matter, I will just stop trying. I will shrink. I will go silent." We retreat into our own personal deserts. We sit down a bowshot away from our lives and just weep, waiting for someone to notice we are gone.

We are starving for a witness. We just want one person to look at us, not at what we do, but at who we are, and say, "I see you. You are doing a good job. You matter."

THE RELEASE

The story of Hagar gives us one of the most powerful theological moments in Scripture.

After the messenger of the Lord speaks to her, after He promises her a future, a son, and a legacy, Hagar looks up and realizes what has just happened. She, a discarded Egyptian slave, has had an encounter with the Creator of the universe.

And in that moment, she gives God a name. She calls Him "El Roi," the God who sees her. She says, in effect, "I have met the One who sees me."

This is the release for you tonight. You are never anonymous to Heaven.

The world may look right through you. Your boss may look past you. Your family may take you for granted. But God sees you.

There is a difference between watching and seeing. A supervisor watches to measure output. A master watches to enforce compliance. But a loving Father sees His daughter.

To be seen in the biblical sense is to be known with understanding, compassion, and recognition.

He saw the moment you swallowed your tears in the bathroom so your children would not see you cry. He saw the extra hour you put into that report that no one read. He saw the way you forgave that friend who did not deserve it. He saw the loneliness you felt when you were surrounded by people.

When Hagar names God El Roi, the One who sees her, she is declaring that her existence is not validated by Abraham or Sarah, not by her labor, and not by her usefulness, but by God alone. She is no one's disposable tool. She is a person held in divine attention.

Notice what God does for her. He does not erase her circumstances overnight. For a season, she still has to return to the tent. The situation remains hard. But she returns changed. She walks back with a steadier spine because she is carrying something no one can take from her. She has been seen by God.

Her visibility to God gives her strength to endure the invisibility of her circumstances.

Then, later, in the second wilderness, God proves it again. He hears the boy's cries. He opens her eyes to water she could not see. He provides for the outcast.

The release is this. You do not need to be the main character to be the beloved. Sarah carries the covenant line and receives the chapters, the miracles, and the lineage. But Hagar receives the encounter. Hagar receives the intimacy of being found.

You might feel like a background character in the story of someone else. But to God, you are the focus of the scene. He is the God of the background. He is the God of the kitchen, the cubicle, the carpool line, and the nursery.

He is the God who sees you, and His eyes are on you right now.

THE INVITATION

When we feel invisible, our tendency is to wait for someone else to validate us. We wait for the "thank you." We wait for the applause. When it does not come, we grow bitter.

Tonight, we are going to break that cycle. We are going to practice witnessing ourselves in the presence of God.

We will use a journal prompt. Writing things down is a way of saying: "This happened. This mattered. I am real."

The "I Am Seen" Journal Prompt

Get a pen and paper. While the notes app on your phone works, paper is often better for focus.

1. **Identify the invisible moment.** Think back over the last twenty four hours. Find one moment where you did something difficult, kind, or exhausting, and no one noticed.
    - Example: I picked up everyone's shoes from the hallway.
    - Example: I stayed calm when the client was yelling at me.
    - Example: I felt incredibly lonely during lunch.
2. **Write it down.** Describe the moment briefly.
3. **Add the stamp.** Next to that sentence, write in all capital letters: GOD SAW ME THEN.

Sit with it. Look at those words. Imagine God standing in the corner of the room in that exact moment, steady and attentive, saying, I saw that. It mattered to me.

You are building a record of your reality. You are reminding yourself that nothing is wasted. Every unseen act of service is held in the memory of God.

BEDTIME PRAYER

The day is done. The audience has gone home, if there ever was one. You are alone in the dark. But you are not invisible.

Whisper these words to the God who has been watching you all day with eyes of love.

God of Hagar, God of the desert, God of the shadows,

I confess that I feel small tonight. I feel used up. I feel like a background character in my own life.

But You are the God who sees me. You saw the work I did today. You saw the tears I swallowed. You saw the love I poured out that was not returned.

You saw the quiet moments no one clapped for. You saw the strength it took to keep going.

I do not need the applause of the world, because I have the attention of the King.

I am not a servant to be discarded. I am a daughter to be cherished.

Watch over me while I sleep. Keep Your eyes on me in the dark.

I am seen. I am known. I am Yours.

Amen.

PART III

THE EXHAUSTION
OF THE SOUL

Stories for when your heart is heavy.

We have explored the exhaustion of the body and the mind. Now, we enter the deepest waters. We enter the exhaustion of the heart.

This section is for the woman who is carrying a grief she cannot put down. It is for the woman whose dreams have been delayed, whose prayers have bounced off the ceiling, and whose hope has become a heavy thing to carry.

We begin with the ache of the empty arms.

7

THE EXHAUSTION OF UNANSWERED PRAYER

THE STORY OF HANNAH (1 SAMUEL 1:1–20)

The Waiting Room

There is a specific kind of exhaustion that does not come from doing too much, but from waiting too long.

It is the exhaustion of hope deferred.

You know this tiredness. It is the feeling of waking up on yet another morning where nothing has changed. The miracle has not happened. The test is still negative. The job offer has not come. The prodigal has not returned. The healing has not manifested.

You are living in the spiritual waiting room.

The waiting room is a brutal place to live. It is quiet, sterile, and suffocating. You sit there, clutching your ticket number and watching the door. You watch other people get called back. You watch friends who started praying after you get their answers before you. You watch people who are not even praying get the very thing you have been begging God for.

And you sit there. And you wait.

This exhaustion creates a fracture in your soul. On one side, you are trying to be a good Christian. You are trying to trust the timing of God. You are trying to say: "Thy will be done." You are trying to be happy for others. But on the other side, there is a rising tide of bitterness. There is confusion. There is the terrifying thought that whispers: "Maybe God has forgotten me. Maybe I am doing it wrong. Maybe He is listening to everyone else, but for me, the line is dead."

It is exhausting to keep your hope alive when reality keeps beating it down. It takes massive amounts of spiritual energy to reinflate a heart that has been punctured by disappointment month after month, year after year.

Eventually, you stop asking. You stop hoping. You do this not because you do not want it, but because you are too tired to survive the crash of another "no."

If you are holding a dream that feels like it is dying, or if you are grieving a "not yet" that feels like a "never," I want you to know: you are not alone in the waiting room. There is a woman sitting in the corner with her head in her hands, her lips moving silently. She knows this pain better than anyone.

Her name is Hannah. She is going to teach us how to pour out a heavy heart without breaking it.

THE IMMERSION

Let us travel to the hill country of Ephraim, and then to the tabernacle at Shiloh.

You are Hannah. And you are defined by what you do not have.

You are married to a husband who loves you. But in a culture where the worth of a woman is measured by her fertility, love is not enough to shield you from shame. Your womb is closed. Scripture says it plainly: the Lord had withheld children from you.

It feels like a divine door slamming shut, a lock with no key.

To make matters worse, you are not the only wife. There is another, Peninnah. Peninnah is fertile. She has sons and daughters. Her tent is full of noise, laughter, and the chaos of childhood.

And Peninnah is cruel. Scripture calls her your adversary. She does not simply enjoy her children. She uses them as weapons against you. She knows exactly where your wound is, and she presses on it again and again.

Day after day, year after year, the provocation continues. You try to hold your head high. You try to ignore her. But the exhaustion of being tormented in your own home wears you down. You feel less than. You feel defective.

The hardest time of the year is the festival at Shiloh. Every year, the family packs up to go to the house of the Lord to sacrifice. This should be a time of celebration. It should be a holiday. But for you, it is a parade of your ache.

Imagine the scene. The family gathers for the ceremonial meal. Your husband, trying to be fair or perhaps trying to compensate, gives portions of meat to Peninnah and to all her sons and daughters. One portion after another. The abundance of Peninnah's life is laid out on the table.

And then he comes to you. He gives you a special portion. It is a gesture of love. He is trying to communicate that you are cherished. But the extra food only highlights the empty chairs around you. You cannot eat. The lump in your throat is too big to swallow.

Peninnah sees it. She leans in and adds another barb. Tears rise fast, hot, familiar. You push the plate away. You lower your head. Humiliation settles over you like a weight.

Your husband sighs. He means well, but he is a fixer. He does not understand the grief of a woman who longs for a child. So he asks why you are weeping, why you will not eat, why your heart is so heavy, and whether his love should be enough to quiet the ache.

Am I not enough?

It is a crushing question. The honest answer is that love cannot replace what you are grieving. He is a good husband, but he cannot fill the specific, aching void in your body and in your dreams. And you cannot say that out loud. So you carry guilt on top of grief. You feel ungrateful. You feel isolated. Even the one who loves you cannot reach the place where you are hurting.

You cannot stay at the table. The laughter of Peninnah's children is like broken glass in your ears. So you stand up. You leave the feast. You walk toward the tabernacle, the tent of meeting where the presence of God dwells.

You are not going there to pray a polite prayer. You are done with polite prayers. You are done with the right words. You are at the breaking point.

You find a spot near the doorway. You fall to your knees, or perhaps you collapse against the wall. You are weeping. But it is not the pretty, single-tear weeping of a movie star. It is the ugly, heaving, shaking sobbing of a soul in agony.

You start to pray. But you are so tired, so choked with emotion, that your voice fails you. You cannot speak out loud. Your lips move, but no sound comes. You are praying from the deepest place inside you, asking God to look on your misery, to remember you, to give you a son. It is the language of the brokenhearted. It is a silent scream.

Then comes the final blow.

Eli, the priest, is sitting by the doorway watching. He sees a woman trembling. He sees her mouth moving but hears no voice. He sees the red eyes and the disheveled appearance, and he assumes the worst. He decides you must be drunk.

So he confronts you and tells you to stop drinking.

Can you imagine the devastation. You have come to God because you have nowhere else to go. You have been tormented by your rival. You have been misunderstood by your husband. And now the representative of God treats you like a shameful spectacle. The one place that should have felt safe becomes another place of judgment.

It is the ultimate exhaustion, the exhaustion of being misunderstood. No one sees you. No one gets it. Not Peninnah, not your husband, not Eli. You are completely alone in your pain.

Or so it seems.

THE CONNECTION

Let us sit in the silence of that temple for a moment.

I know there are women reading this who know the specific pain of Hannah: the pain of infertility. I know the exhaustion of the two-week wait. The exhaustion of tracking ovulation, of shots and hormones, and of negative tests that feel like a death every single month. I know the exhaustion of seeing pregnancy announcements on social media and feeling that immediate, involuntary stab of jealousy, followed by the wave of guilt for not being happy for them. I know the exhaustion of people saying: "Just relax and it will happen." or "Why don't you just adopt?" These words feel like the rebuke of Eli, dismissing the complexity of your pain.

But the story of Hannah is not just about babies. It is about the longing.

It is the longing of the single woman who is tired of being a bridesmaid while waiting for her own love story. It is the longing of the professional who is qualified, prepared, and faithful, but keeps watching doors stay shut. It is the longing of the grieving wife who is tired of praying for her husband's heart to soften. It is the longing of the sick who wakes up day after day in a body that has not found its miracle yet.

This is the exhaustion of the unanswered prayer.

It is the fatigue of keeping your hands raised when your arms are cramping. It is the bitterness that starts to taste like metal in your mouth. It is the question that keeps you awake at night: "Why her and not me?"

Like Hannah, you often feel you must hide this pain. You cannot weep at the dinner table or you will ruin the mood. You cannot tell your husband, your friends, or family the truth, because they will try to fix it with platitudes. You cannot tell the priest or the church, because they might judge you for lacking faith.

So you carry it alone. You bottle it up. You create a dam inside your soul to hold back the river of grief. And holding back that river is the most exhausting thing you will ever do.

THE RELEASE

But look at what Hannah does.

When Eli assumes she is drunk, something steadies in her. She does not run away in shame. She does not collapse into apologies. She defends her grief.

She tells him she has not been drinking. She explains that she is deeply troubled, and that what he is seeing is not intoxication, but anguish. She has been praying from the depths, pouring out her soul before the Lord.

Poured out her soul.

This is the key. This is the release. Hannah does not offer a polished, structured prayer. She does not reach for a formula. She brings her whole self. She treats her soul like a pitcher and tips it until it is empty.

She pours out the bitterness. She pours out the jealousy stirred by Peninnah. She pours out the frustration that her husband cannot fix. She pours out her confusion toward God. She pours out the ugly, raw, unfiltered truth.

She does not sanitize her pain before she brings it to the Lord. She brings the pain as it is.

Notice what happens next. Eli recognizes his mistake. He blesses her and sends her away in peace, asking the God of Israel to grant what she has been praying for.

Then Scripture gives us a detail that changes the whole scene. Hannah returns to the meal. She eats. And her face is no longer marked by the same despair.

Stop and think about that. She is still childless in that moment. She has not conceived yet. She still has to return to the same household with the same rival. Her circumstances have not shifted.

But she has.

Her face changes because she is no longer carrying the weight alone. She has poured it out. She has handed the burden over. She has been honest in the presence of God, and that honesty has made room for breath again.

The release for you tonight is this. Prayer is not about performing the right words to unlock the outcome you want. Prayer is about being honest enough to survive what you are living through.

God can handle your bitterness. He can handle your jealousy. He can handle your disappointment. He is not fragile. You do not have to protect Him from your real emotions.

If you are exhausted, it may be because you are trying to pray beautiful prayers while holding back a tidal wave of truth. You are trying to say "thank you" when what is rising in you is "where are You?" The effort of swallowing that cry will wear you down.

God invites you to do what Hannah did. Pour it out. Tip the pitcher over. Let the heavy sediment at the bottom come up and out. Tell Him you are angry. Tell Him you are jealous. Tell Him you are tired of waiting.

There is a peace that comes not only from receiving the answer, but from being fully known. Hannah found peace before she found Samuel. She found appetite before she found conception.

The release is the pouring out.

THE INVITATION

We often treat our tears like something to be ashamed of. We apologize for crying. We wipe them away quickly. We try to compose ourselves. But in the ancient world, tears were seen as a liquid form of prayer. Psalm 56 says that God puts our tears into His bottle. He keeps them. They are precious to Him.

Tonight, we are going to practice a ritual of release. We are going to stop wiping the tears away.

The "Pour Out" Ritual

1. **Find your sanctuary.** Just like Hannah found a spot by the doorpost, find a place where you can be alone: your car, the shower, a closet, or the side of your bed.
2. **Access the ache.** Think about the thing you are waiting for. The "not yet." Let yourself feel the unfairness of it. Let yourself feel the sadness. Do not preach to yourself. Do not jump to "God is good." Just stay in the "this hurts."
3. **Let the tears come.** If they come, let them.
4. **The Rule.** Do not wipe them. This is the hard part. Your reflex will be to wipe your cheeks. Do not. Let the tears roll down your face. Let them drip off your chin. Let them fall onto your hands or your lap.

5. **The Offering.** Imagine that those tears are the liquid of your soul pouring out. As they fall, say or think: "I pour this out. I pour this out. I am not keeping this inside anymore."
6. **The Transfer.** When the tears stop, visualize that the weight of that grief is now in a puddle on the floor, at the feet of Jesus. It is outside of you. He is holding it now.

You can wash your face afterward. But for that moment, let the mess be the message.

BEDTIME PRAYER

The feast is over. The taunts of Peninnah are silenced by the night. You have wept. You have poured. Now, you can rest.

Whisper these words to the God who hears the silent scream.

God of Shiloh, God of the waiting room, God of the closed womb and the open ear,

I confess that I am bitter. I confess that I am jealous. I confess that I am tired of watching everyone else feast while I starve.

Tonight, I stop pretending I am okay. I stop trying to pray polite prayers. I pour out my soul to You.

Here is my longing. Here is my grief. Here is my confusion. I tip the pitcher over until it is empty.

I give you the weight of the "not yet." I trade my heaviness for Your peace. I may not have the answer yet, but I have You.

And You are better to me than ten sons. You are better to me than the dream.

I leave my burden at the doorpost. I go to sleep in peace.

Amen.

8

THE EXHAUSTION OF GRIEF
THE STORY OF NAOMI (RUTH 1–4)

The Fog of the Empty Chair

There is an exhaustion that has no cure in sleep. It is not the tiredness of overworked muscles or the fatigue of an overtaxed mind. It is a cellular heaviness. It is the feeling that gravity has suddenly tripled, pulling you down into the earth.

This is the exhaustion of grief.

It is the specific, crushing fatigue of living in the aftermath of a loss.

When we talk about grief, we often talk about the emotions: the sadness, the anger, and the shock. But we rarely talk about the physical toll. We rarely talk about the "grief fog," which is the way your brain seems to be wrapped in cotton wool, making simple tasks like boiling water or signing a check feel like advanced calculus. We do not talk about the way grief suppresses the immune system, leaving you vulnerable and weak. We do not talk about the sheer caloric expense of getting out of bed when your heart is broken.

I am speaking to the woman who has lost a person. I am speaking to the widow who reaches for a hand that is not there in the middle of the night. I am speaking to the mother who has walked away from a graveside. I am speaking to the daughter who has deleted a phone number she can no longer call.

But I am also speaking to the woman who is grieving a living loss. This might be the divorce that wrecked the future you had planned, or the career that crumbled after decades of building. Perhaps it is the friendship that dissolved into silence, the diagnosis that changed the trajectory of your life, or the dream that you finally had to admit is never going to happen.

This exhaustion is profound because it is the exhaustion of emptiness. You are carrying the weight of an absence. Paradoxically, the missing thing is heavier than the thing itself ever was. The silence in the house is louder than the noise ever was.

In this state, the most exhausting thing of all is the pressure to be okay. The world has a stopwatch on grief. People give you a week, maybe a month, of casseroles and sympathy cards. Then, they expect you to move on. They expect you to find the silver lining or to triumph over the tragedy.

So you fake it. You put on the mask of the "Strong Survivor." You say, "I am doing okay," because you do not want to make other people uncomfortable with your pain. You smile when you want to scream. You stand up when you want to collapse.

That acting job is draining the very last drops of your life force.

Tonight, we are going to walk a dusty road with a woman who refused to fake it. She is one of the most honest women in the Bible. She did not put on a happy face for the neighbors. She did not offer platitudes about the plan of God. She looked the world in the eye and said: "I am bitter."

Her name was Naomi. She is going to show us that the path to rest begins with telling the truth about our pain

THE IMMERSION

Let us go to the high plains of Moab.

It is a foreign land. The wind here blows differently than it does at home. The gods they worship here are strange. The soil looks different.

You are Naomi. And you are standing in a cemetery.

Ten years ago, you came to this place with a full life. You came with a husband. You came with two young sons. You were refugees, fleeing a famine in Bethlehem, looking for bread. You thought this would be a temporary stop. You thought you would survive here.

But Moab has become a graveyard.

First, your husband died. The pillar of your life was buried in foreign soil. You were left a widow, which was a vulnerable and dangerous thing to be in the ancient world. But you survived. You still had your sons. You watched them grow. You watched them marry local women. You pinned all your hopes on the next generation. Grandchildren, you thought, would be the healing.

Then the unthinkable happened. One son died. Then the other.

Both of them are gone. There are no grandchildren, no heirs, and no husband. You are left with three graves and two daughters-in-law who are now widows themselves.

Stand there for a moment in the silence of that house. Imagine the deafening quiet. The table that used to seat four is now empty. The future you built, the lineage, the security, the protection, has been wiped away.

You are not just sad. You are hollowed out. You are a shell of a woman.

Then you hear a rumor. The famine in Bethlehem is over. The Lord has come to the aid of His people by providing food.

So you decide to go home. You do not go because you feel hopeful, but because you have nowhere else to go. You cannot stay in the land of your dead.

You pack your meager belongings. You tell your daughters-in-law to go back to their mothers. You try to push them away. Why should they be tethered to a dead end.

One leaves, weeping. But Ruth refuses to go. She clings to you. She vows to follow you. You are too tired to argue. If she wants to walk with a woman who feels half alive, let her come.

Now the journey begins. The road from Moab to Bethlehem is not a short walk. It is a trek. It involves descending into the Jordan Valley, where the air is hot and heavy, and then climbing up the rugged limestone ridges of Judah.

Feel the dust on your face. Feel the ache in your legs. Every step is a battle against gravity. Every step is a reminder of who is not walking beside you.

You remember walking this road ten years ago, leaving Bethlehem. You were worried about food then, but you were surrounded by your family. You were a wife. You were a mother. You were full.

Now you are walking back with empty hands. The physical exhaustion of the miles is matched only by the spiritual exhaustion of the return. You know what awaits you in Bethlehem. You fear the whispers, the pitying looks, and the questions about where your husband is, where your sons are, and what happened to you.

You dread the arrival more than the journey. You dread the moment you must face the life you left behind and show people the wreckage of what you have become.

Finally, the town comes into view. It looks the same. The stone houses, the threshing floors, the olive trees. And the smell of baking bread drifts through the air because the famine is indeed over. Everyone else is eating. Everyone else is celebrating.

As you walk through the gates, a murmur runs through the crowd. The women of the town, perhaps the friends of your youth, gather around. They squint in the sunlight. They take in your lined face, your dusty clothes, your stooped posture.

They can hardly believe it is you.

Your name means pleasant. Sweet. Lovely. It was the name of a young bride. It was the name of a mother with a full house.

Hearing that name now feels like a slap. It feels like a lie. There is nothing pleasant about your life. There is nothing sweet about burying a husband and two sons. To be called Naomi feels like a mockery of your pain.

Something rises up in your throat. The raw, jagged truth. You are too tired to be polite. You are too tired to pretend.

So you stop them. You look them in the eye. And you tell them not to call you pleasant anymore.

You tell them to call you Mara instead, because bitterness has filled your life.

You tell them you left Bethlehem full, and you have returned empty. You say that the Lord has dealt harshly with you, that the Almighty has brought affliction upon you.

The silence that follows must have been thick. You did not merely say you were sad. You spoke your grief toward God without softening the edges.

You stand there in the town square, stripped of your husband, your sons, and even your sense of self. You are the empty woman.

Then you walk to your old, crumbling house, and you collapse into the dark.

THE CONNECTION

Let us sit in the dark with Naomi for a while.

Her words are uncomfortable, are they not. She says that the Almighty has dealt bitterly with her.

We are not used to hearing women speak like that in church. We are taught to be the Proverbs 31 woman, strong, smiling, clothed in strength and dignity. We are taught to repeat what is safe and approved, even when our world is burning down.

But I suspect there is a part of you that resonates deeply with the name Mara.

This is for the woman who has lost a child and feels a flash of anger every time she sees a baby shower invitation. This is for the woman who was faithful in her marriage, only to be betrayed, and now must sign divorce papers she never wanted. This is for the woman who worked for twenty years to build a business, only to lose it in a recession. This is for the woman staring at a cancer diagnosis, wondering why God did not protect her.

This is the exhaustion of the mask.

You are tired of pretending you are not angry. You are tired of pretending everything happens for a reason. You are tired of people trying to add a bright ending to a story that is still bleeding.

Grief is bitter. Loss is bitter. Emptiness is bitter. When we try to sugarcoat it, when we force ourselves to be Naomi when we are actually Mara, something fractures inside. We start to distance ourselves from God, not because we do not believe, but because we do not know how to be honest.

You think if you tell God you are angry, He will punish you. You think if you admit you are bitter, you are a bad Christian.

So you carry the grief alone. You play the role of the faithful sufferer. You say the right verses. But inside, you are unraveling. You are exhausted from holding up the heavy ceiling of your grief so it does not fall on the people around you.

You feel empty. And the worst part of the emptiness is the fear that God has turned His back on you. Naomi did not simply feel unlucky. She felt singled out. She felt that the One who could have spared her family did not.

That is a terrifying, lonely place to be. If you are there tonight, I want you to know you do not have to leave. Not yet. You do not have to fix it tonight.

THE RELEASE

Here is the most stunning part of the story of Naomi. It is actually what does not happen.

Naomi stands in the middle of Bethlehem and screams at God. She calls Him her afflicter. She changes her name to Bitter. She essentially resigns from hope.

And do you know what God does?

Does lightning strike her? No. Does a prophet come out and rebuke her for her lack of faith? No. Does the ground open up and swallow her? No.

God listens. He lets her say it. He lets her be Mara. He allows the lament to hang in the air without correction.

This is the first release: God is not intimidated by your grief. He is not offended by your bitterness. He knows that bitterness is just the crust that forms over a deep, bleeding wound. He is big enough to handle your anger. You can tell Him the truth. You can be Mara for a season.

There is a second, quieter release.

While Naomi is declaring she has come back empty, she is not actually empty. She is saying, in her grief, that the Lord has brought her home with nothing left. But who is standing right beside her as she says it?

Ruth was standing right there.

Ruth was the young, strong, loyal daughter-in-law who had pledged her life to Naomi. Ruth was the one who would go into the fields to glean barley to keep them alive. Ruth would eventually marry Boaz and give birth to Obed.

Obed would be the father of Jesse. Jesse would be the father of David. And from the line of David would come Jesus.

Do you see it? In the exact moment Naomi was shouting, "I have nothing!" the seed of the Messiah was standing right beside her. In the exact moment she felt abandoned by God, God was already at work, weaving the lineage of the Savior through her family.

Naomi could not see it. And God did not force her to see it yet. He did not make Ruth announce herself as a blessing. He let Naomi be grief stricken. He let her sleep. He let her mourn. But He kept working in the background.

This is the theology of background redemption. When you are exhausted by grief, you cannot see the future. You cannot see the plan. You cannot see the good. You can only see the grave. And that is not a failure. You do not have to see it for it to be true.

God does not require you to be optimistic while you are grieving. He does not require you to have vision when you are in the dark.

He is working while you weep. He is planting seeds in winter that you will not recognize until spring. He is moving pieces you cannot yet name, the harvest, the field, the family redeemer, the quiet provision, while you are simply trying to make it through another day.

Naomi thought her life was over. She thought the story ended at the cemetery in Moab. But God knew the story was still unfolding in Bethlehem.

In time, joy returned. Scripture tells us that when Ruth gave birth, the women of the town gathered around Naomi. They placed the baby in her arms. They blessed the Lord for providing a redeemer for the family, and they spoke hope over Naomi's future, saying this child would renew her life and sustain her in her old age.

Naomi held the baby. The emptiness began to fill. The bitterness softened under the weight of new life. She cared for the child and found purpose again.

But she did not find it by striving. She found it by surviving. She kept waking up. She let Ruth walk beside her. She kept taking the next step until the season changed.

The release for you tonight is this. You do not have to manufacture your own redemption. You do not have to force your grief to resolve on command. You only have to let God carry you through the dark. You can be empty. He is full enough for both of you.

THE INVITATION

We often think that prayer must be polite. We think we have to clean up our emotions before we bring them to the King. But the Psalms are full of people yelling at God. It is called lament.

Lament is not a sin. Lament is an act of trust. It is trusting God enough to tell Him the ugly truth. It is believing that He is strong enough to hold your pain.

Tonight, we are going to do something brave. We are going to stop being Naomi for a moment, and we are going to be Mara. We are going to get the poison out.

The "Lament List"

1. **Find a piece of paper.** Or open a note on your phone. Write the title: "Things That Hurt."
2. **List three things.** I want you to write down three things that are causing you pain right now.
3. **The Rule.** You are not allowed to spiritualize them. You are not allowed to add a "God won't give you more than you can handle" at the end. Just write the raw pain.
   - Example: "I am angry that my husband left me and I hate seeing pictures of him happy."
   - Example: "I am pissed that I lost my job. I hate having to worry about money and I am embarrassed if I cannot do things that cost money with my friends."
   - Example: "I am lonely and I feel forgotten."
4. **Read them out loud to God.** Whisper them. Say: "God, this is my truth right now. I am giving it to You."
5. **Leave it.** Do not try to fix it. Just let the list exist. You have told the truth. That is enough.

By doing this, you are acknowledging that you are empty. And it is into the empty vessels that God pours His oil.

BEDTIME PRAYER

The road back to Bethlehem is long, and you are tired. You have carried the name Mara all day. Tonight, let God hold the weight of your name.

Whisper these words into the silence of your room.

> *God of the Grieving, God of the Empty, God of the Long Road Home,*
>
> *I confess that I am tired of pretending. I am tired of the mask of "pleasant." I feel the bitterness of loss. I feel the ache of the empty room.*

Tonight, I stop trying to be strong. I admit that I am empty. I admit that I cannot see the redemption yet.

Thank You that You do not rebuke my grief. Thank You that You are working in the background while I weep. Thank You for the Ruths in my life: the blessings I am too tired to see.

I give You my emptiness. I give You my broken heart. Redeem my life while I sleep.

I am not alone. I am not forgotten. I am held.

Amen.

9

THE EXHAUSTION OF WORRY

THE STORY OF MARY, MOTHER OF JESUS (LUKE 2; JOHN 19)

The Night Shift of the Heart

There is a job description that comes with motherhood, or with loving anyone deeply, that no one warns you about. It is the position of the Watchman.

You know this role. It is the part of you that never really sleeps. Even when your body is unconscious, your ear is tuned to the frequency of a cough, a cry, or the sound of the front door opening.

This is the exhaustion of worry.

It is the exhaustion of hyper-vigilance. It is the fatigue of trying to predict the future so you can prevent pain. It is the mental labor of playing out every worst case scenario in your head, believing that if you can just imagine the disaster vividly enough, you can somehow stop it from happening.

I am speaking to the mother of the toddler, who sees every sharp corner, every open outlet, and every stranger as a threat. You are exhausted because you are standing between your child and a dangerous world, twenty-four hours a day.

I am speaking to the mother of the teenager who lies awake until she hears the tires in the driveway. You are exhausted by how little control you have. You cannot protect them from a broken heart, a cruel text message, or a tragic accident. Every time they walk out the door, it feels like your heart is walking around outside your body, and it is terrifying.

I am speaking to the mother of the adult child, who sees the bad relationship, the financial struggle, or the drift away from faith. You are exhausted by the silence. You cannot fix it anymore. You can only watch.

I am speaking to anyone who loves someone vulnerable. The wife of the police officer. The daughter of the aging parent. The friend of the addict.

This exhaustion is heavy because it is built on a terrifying realization: I cannot save them.

We think that if we worry enough, we can control the outcome. We think worry is a form of love. If I worry, it means I care. If I stop worrying, it means I am negligent. So we carry the burden of the entire world on our shoulders, terrified that if we shrug it off for even a second, everything will crumble.

But worry does not empty tomorrow of its sorrow; it only empties today of its strength.

Tonight, we are going to look at the woman who had more reason to worry than any mother in history. She was given the task of raising God in a world that wanted to kill Him. She lived with a prophecy of doom hanging over her head for thirty-three years.

Her name was Mary. She knows what it feels like to have to let go of the person you love most.

THE IMMERSION

Let us go to the Temple in Jerusalem.

You are Mary. You are young, perhaps only fourteen or fifteen. You are tired. You have just traveled the long road from Bethlehem. You have survived childbirth in a stable. You have survived the strangeness of shepherds and angels.

Now, you are standing in the chaotic, noisy courts of the Temple to dedicate your son. You hold Him in your arms. He is eight days old. He is warm, small, and fragile. You can feel His heartbeat against your chest. The smell of milk and new skin is intoxicating.

You are doing what every mother does: you are dreaming of His future. You are counting His fingers. You are marveling at the perfection of His eyelashes. You feel that fierce, lioness instinct rising in your gut: I will let nothing hurt you. I will die before I let anything touch you.

An old man approaches. His name is Simeon. He looks at your baby with eyes full of tears and glory. He praises God. Your heart swells with pride.

Then his expression shifts. The warmth does not disappear, but it deepens into something sober. He looks at the child, and then he looks directly at you. And he tells you that this baby will not be harmless.

He says your son will be the turning point for many in Israel, causing some to fall and others to rise. He will be opposed and spoken against. And then Simeon chooses a specific image. He says that what is coming for your son will not stop with him. It will reach you too. He describes it as a sword that will pierce your own soul.

The air leaves the room. A sword. Not a crown. Not a blessing. A sword.

You look down at the sleeping infant. You wrap the blanket tighter. A sword? What does that mean? When will it come? Will it be sickness? Will it be war? Will it be an accident?

From that moment on, the shadow appears. You take Him home. You nurse Him. You rock Him to sleep. But the words are always there, hovering in the corner of the nursery. A sword will pierce your soul.

Every time He falls and scrapes His knee, your heart stops: Is this the sword? Every time the soldiers of King Herod march nearby, you hide Him: Is this the sword? Every time He gets a fever, you sit up all night, watching His chest rise and fall: Is this the sword?

You become the ultimate watchman. You are raising a target. You are trying to protect a secret that the world is not ready for. The burden of vigilance is crushing.

Fast forward twelve years.

You are on the road back from Passover. The caravan is huge, filled with cousins, uncles, and neighbors. The noise of travel is loud. You assume He is with Joseph. Joseph assumes He is with you. You travel for a whole day. As the sun sets, you look for Him at the campfire. No one has seen Him since morning.

The cold ice of panic floods your veins. It is a physical sickness. I lost Him. God gave me one job, to protect His Son, and I lost Him.

You turn around. You run back toward Jerusalem. The journey that took a day to walk takes forever in your mind. The sun goes down. It is dark. The road is dangerous. Where is He? Is He cold? Is He hungry? Has someone taken Him? The what-if scenarios scream in your head. What if He is hurt? What if the soldiers found Him? What if the sword is here?

You search for three days. Three days of no sleep. Three days of tearing through the crowds, grabbing strangers, describing His face. Your voice is hoarse from screaming His name. You are hysterical with grief. You are living the worst nightmare of every parent.

Then you find Him. He is in the Temple, sitting calmly among the teachers, listening and asking questions. He looks up at you, safe and unafraid.

You rush to Him. You pull Him close. You want to shake Him and hold Him at the same time. You ask why He has done this to you, why He would let you suffer like this, and you tell Him that you and Joseph have been searching for Him in deep distress.

You were not looking with mild concern. You were searching in agony.

And He meets your fear with a steadiness that feels suddenly older than twelve. He asks why you were searching, as if the answer should have been clear. He reminds you that He must be in His Father's house, doing what His Father has sent Him to do.

It hits you then. He is not yours to keep. He has another Father. He has another home. He has a mission you cannot manage. You cannot tuck Him safely into your plans. You cannot protect Him from His calling, even if His calling terrifies you. You have to let Him grow. You have to let Him go.

Fast forward.

Now the sword arrives.

You are standing on a hill called Golgotha. The sky has gone dark. The air tastes like blood and vinegar. You lift your eyes and there He is. Your baby. The one you rocked. The one you nursed. The one you searched for through the streets.

He is stripped and beaten. He is dying. And you cannot fix it. There is no bandage for this. No comfort you can offer that will undo it. You cannot appeal to the authorities, because the authorities are the ones doing it. You are powerless.

This is the piercing Simeon spoke of. The moment you learn that a mother's love, no matter how fierce, is not a shield. You cannot stop the world from breaking your child.

You stand there and you do not look away. You keep vigil. And with a breaking heart, you face the truth that the only way for Him to fulfill His purpose is for you to release your grip.

You have to give Him back to the Father. You have to trust that the Father loves Him even more than you do. You have to trust that resurrection is coming, even when this day at the cross feels like it is undoing you.

THE CONNECTION

Let us leave the foot of the cross and come back to your bedroom, where you are staring at the baby monitor or checking your phone for a text.

The distance between you and Mary is not as far as you think. You, too, have felt the prophecy of the sword.

From the moment the nurse placed that baby in your arms, you felt it: the terrifying vulnerability. You realized that your heart was now walking around outside your body, exposed to traffic, to viruses, to bullies, and to heartbreak.

This chapter is for the Safety Mom. You are the one who researches every car seat. You obsess over ingredients. You track the fever curve. You are terrified of choking, of falls, and of accidents. You think, "If I am just vigilant enough, I can keep them alive." But deep down, you know that you are one distracted driver away from tragedy, and that lack of control keeps you awake.

This chapter is for the Social Mom. You worry about their heart. You worry that they are lonely at school. You worry about the mean girls. You worry that they are not making friends. You want to go to the playground and fight their battles for them. You want to wrap them in bubble wrap so they never feel rejection. But you know you cannot. You have to watch them walk into the school building alone.

This chapter is for the Future Mom. You worry about their choices. Will they get into college? Who will they marry? Are they making a mistake? You see the path they are walking, and you see the cliffs, and you are screaming at them to turn around, but they cannot hear you, or they will not listen. You feel the panic Mary felt in Jerusalem: I lost Him. I lost the connection.

This is for the Prodigal Mom. Your child has walked away. Maybe into addiction. Maybe into a lifestyle you fear. Maybe just into silence. You are standing at the window, waiting. You are bargaining with God. Keep them safe. Bring them home. The sword is piercing your soul every single day.

The exhaustion comes because you are trying to be God. I say that gently. We try to be omnipresent, watching them always. We try to be omniscient, knowing everything they do. We try to be omnipotent, fixing every problem.

But we are human. We need sleep. We have limits. When we try to carry a God-sized burden with human-sized shoulders, we break.

The lie of worry is this: "If I let go, they will fall." The truth of faith is this: "If I let go, God will catch them."

THE RELEASE

The life of Mary was a series of releases. She had to release Him to the shepherds. She had to release Him to the Temple teachers. She had to release Him to His ministry, watching Him walk away from her home in Nazareth to be homeless and hunted. She had to release Him to the cross.

But here is the anchor for your soul tonight: Mary did not save Jesus.

Mary's worry did not save Him. Her chicken soup did not save Him. Her protection did not save Him. The Father saved Him.

But God saved Him through the darkness, not from it.

This is the hardest spiritual truth for a mother to accept: the plan of God for your child might involve a valley. It might involve a failure. It might involve a heartbreak. It might involve a sword.

If God the Father allowed His own Son to go through the cross to get to the Resurrection, He might allow your child to go through a struggle to get to their redemption.

Your job is not to be the Messiah for your children. Your job is to point them to the Messiah. Your job is not to prevent their story from having conflict. Your job is to trust the Author of the story.

The release comes when you realize that God loves your children more than you do.

I know that sounds impossible. You carried them. You birthed them. You would die for them. But God created them. He knit them together. He numbered their days before one of them came to be. His investment in them is infinite. His plans for them are eternal.

You are the bow. They are the arrow. You can polish the arrow. You can aim the arrow. You can pull the string back with all your might. But eventually, for the arrow to fulfill its purpose, you have to let go of the string. You have to let it fly into a wind that you cannot control.

Mary stood at the cross, and she let go. She surrendered her right to fix it. She surrendered her right to understand it. She simply stood there and let God be God.

Three days later, the tomb was empty. The story did not end in the dark. And the story is not over for your child, either.

THE INVITATION

Tonight, we are going to do a visualization. Our minds are powerful. We often use our imagination to visualize disaster. Tonight, we are going to use it to visualize surrender.

This is a way to physically signal to your brain that you are going off duty.

The "Release" Visualization

1. **Close your eyes.** Get comfortable. Take a deep breath. Imagine the shore. Picture yourself standing on the edge of a calm, vast lake. It is twilight. The water is still.
2. **The Boat.** At your feet, bobbing in the shallow water, is a small, wooden boat. It is sturdy and safe.
3. **Place the worry.** I want you to imagine taking the person you are worried about, your child, your spouse, or your friend. Or, if that feels too scary, imagine taking the specific worry, the fear of the accident or the fear of the future, packaged as a heavy box. Gently place them, or the box, into the boat. Make sure they are comfortable. Make sure the package is secure.
4. **See Jesus.** Look out onto the water. A few yards away, Jesus is standing there. Or perhaps He is in another boat nearby. He is waiting. He is smiling. He looks strong.
5. **The Push.** This is the hard part. I want you to visualize yourself bending down, placing your hands on the bow of the boat, and giving it a gentle push. Feel the wood leave your hands. Watch the boat drift away from the shore.
6. **The Transfer.** Watch the boat drift toward Jesus. See Him reach out and catch the line. See Him pull the boat close to Him. He has it now. He is holding the boat. You are standing on the shore, empty-handed. Whisper: "They are safe on the water with You."

You are not abandoning them. You are transferring them from your limited care to His infinite care.

BEDTIME PRAYER

You have been the watchman all day. But the shift is over. The other Watchman, the One who neither slumbers nor sleeps, is here to take over.

Whisper these words to the God who loves your children best.

God of Mary, God of the Temple, God of the Cross and the Empty Tomb,

I confess that I am exhausted by worry. I am tired of trying to control the future. I am tired of playing out the disasters in my mind. I am tired of the sword hanging over my head.

Tonight, I resign as the General Manager of the Universe. I acknowledge that I cannot save the people I love. I cannot protect them from every fall.

So I place them in the boat. I push them onto the water of Your grace. You are the Father. You are the Shepherd. You are the Savior.

I trust Your love more than my fear. I trust Your plan more than my control.

Hold them while I sleep. Keep watch while I rest.

They are Yours. They are Yours. They are Yours.

Amen.

10

THE EXHAUSTION
OF THE UNKNOWN

THE STORY OF RUTH (RUTH 1–4)

The Fog of the Future

We have arrived at the final exhaustion. It is perhaps the most paralyzing of them all. It is the exhaustion of standing on the edge of a cliff, looking out into a thick, gray fog, and having no idea where the bridge is.

This is the exhaustion of the unknown.

It is the fatigue of the in-between. You have left the old life, or the old life has kicked you out, but you have not arrived at the new life yet. You are in transition. You are in the hallway between two doors.

I am speaking to the woman who is starting over. Perhaps you are navigating life after a divorce. The map you had for your future, the shared retirement and the growing old together, has been burned in a fire you did not start. You are looking at a blank canvas, and it does not feel like freedom; it feels like terrifying emptiness.

Perhaps you are moving to a new city where you do not know a soul. You are staring at cardboard boxes, wondering if you will ever feel at home again. You are tired of using GPS to find the grocery store. You are tired of being a stranger.

Perhaps you are standing at the edge of a career shift. The industry you worked in for 15 years has changed, you have been laid off, or you simply cannot do it anymore. So you scroll through online job postings, and the impostor syndrome starts to rise. You catch yourself thinking, "Will anyone even hire me now? Will they see my experience as value, or as a reason to pass me over?"

Or maybe you are in a season of spiritual fog. You used to hear God clearly. You used to feel steady, like you knew the way forward. But now the sky feels silent. You cannot see the next step, and the uncertainty has you turning in circles, afraid that one wrong move will cost you everything.

This exhaustion comes from decision fatigue. When everything is up in the air, every single choice feels heavy. Where should I live? What should I spend? Who should I trust? Is this the right school? Is this the right doctor? Your brain is working overtime, trying to be the architect, the builder, and the safety inspector of your life all at once.

You are exhausted because you are trying to solve a puzzle with half the pieces missing. You are trying to guarantee a safe landing before you have even jumped.

We live in a culture that worships the five-year plan. We are told to manifest our destiny, to set goals, and to visualize the outcome. But what happens when you cannot see the outcome? What happens when the path is dark?

Tonight, we are going to walk with a woman who had no map. She left everything she knew to walk into a hostile land with nothing but the clothes on her back and a promise to a bitter mother-in-law.

Her name was Ruth. She is going to teach us the secret of resting in the dark.

THE IMMERSION

Let us go back to the dusty road on the border of Moab.

You are Ruth. You are young, but you feel old. You have already lived a lifetime of grief. You married a foreigner and you buried him. You are a widow before your life has even truly begun.

You are standing at a crossroads. Behind you is Moab. It is home. It is familiar. It is where your parents live. It is where your gods are worshipped. It is where the food tastes right and the customs make sense. If you turn back, you know exactly what your life will look like. It will be safe. It will be predictable.

In front of you is Judah. It is a foreign land: a land of mountains and strange laws. It is a land where you are the enemy. The Israelites do not like Moabites. To them, you are unclean. You are unwanted. Walking that road means choosing poverty. It means choosing permanent outsider status. It means clinging to an old woman, Naomi, who has nothing to offer you but her own bitterness.

Your sister-in-law, Orpah, kisses Naomi and turns back. She chooses what is familiar. No one blames her. It is the sensible choice.

But you feel something in your chest pulling you forward. Not reason. Not comfort. A strange, steady gravity that will not let you go. You cling to Naomi. You look into her tired, grief-stricken face, and you make a vow that echoes through history.

You tell her you are not leaving. Where she goes, you will go. Where she stays, you will stay. Her people will become your people. Her God will become your God.

You say it out loud, and it sounds simple for a moment.

Then the reality settles in.

You have just cut yourself loose from the life you knew. You have stepped away from your old name, your old safety, your old future.

You are walking into uncertainty with nothing but a promise on your tongue.

You are free-falling.

You arrive in Bethlehem. The town is buzzing with the barley harvest. Everyone knows everyone. Families are reuniting. Laughter spills out of the houses. But not for you. You are the Moabitess. You hear the whisper every time you pass. You see the side-eyes. You are the strange girl trailing behind the bitter widow.

You have no husband to provide for you. You have no money. You have no social standing. Hunger is a real and present danger. Naomi is too old to work. If you do not find food, you both starve.

So, you have to do the most humiliating task in the ancient world: gleaning.

Gleaning is the welfare system of Israel. The law states that farmers must not harvest the corners of their fields, or pick up the stalks they drop, so that the poor and the foreigner can follow behind and pick them up. It is back-breaking work. It involves walking bent over all day, scavenging for scraps in the dirt. It puts you at the mercy of the field hands, rough men who might harass you or chase you away.

Imagine the first morning. You wake up before the sun. You wrap your shawl tight. You step out into the unknown. You do not know which field is safe. You do not know where to go. You just start walking. Your heart is hammering. What if they yell at me? What if I come home empty-handed? What if I made a terrible mistake coming here?

You find a field. You start to work. The sun beats down on your neck. The barley stalks scratch your hands. Your back screams in protest. You are thirsty, but you do not dare drink from the water jars reserved for the workers. You keep your head down. You work. You pick up one stalk. Then another. Then another.

You do not know that this is the field of Boaz. You do not know that he is a wealthy relative. You do not know that he is watching you. You do not know that this moment is the turning point of your destiny.

All you know is the heat. All you know is the hunger. All you know is the next stalk of grain.

Fast forward to the end of the harvest. Naomi gives you a strange instruction. She tells you to wash, put on perfume, and go down to the threshing floor where Boaz is working late, tossing the barley into the air so the wind can blow the chaff away. She tells you to wait until he is asleep, and then lie down at his feet.

In our modern ears, this sounds odd. In that culture, it was terrifying. The threshing floor at night was a place of men. It was dangerous. The act of uncovering his feet was a symbolic proposal, a quiet plea for covering and protection. You are asking him to be your family redeemer, the one with the right and responsibility to step in and shelter you.

You are risking everything. If he wakes up and is offended, he could have you beaten. He could publicly shame you. He could banish you from the fields. You would be ruined.

Imagine the walk to the threshing floor in the dark. The air is cool. The smell of chaff and grain is thick. The stars are bright above the hills of Judah. You are trembling. You do not know the outcome. You have no guarantee. You are walking purely on trust: trust in Naomi, and a tentative trust in the God of Israel.

You creep into the space. You see him sleeping. You lie down at his feet. And you wait. You lie there in the dark, heart racing, staring at the sky. What will happen when he wakes? Will he reject me? Will he accept me? What is my future?

You have absolutely no control over what happens next. You have played your part. Now, you must wait in the dark. This is the ultimate posture of the unknown: lying still at the feet of the Redeemer, waiting for the morning.

THE CONNECTION

Let us come back to your life.

You might not be gleaning barley, but you are gleaning for answers. You are waking up every day, going to the computer, searching for jobs, searching for houses, and searching for a sign. You are working hard, picking up scraps of information, and trying to piece together a future.

You are exhausted because you cannot see the harvest. You can only see the stalks in your hand right now.

This chapter is for the woman in the corridor. You have shut the door behind you. You have left the toxic relationship, the dead-end job, or the city that did not fit. But the door in front of you has not opened yet. You are standing in the dark hallway. And the fear is whispering: "You made a mistake. You should have stayed in Moab. At least in Moab, you knew what to expect. At least in Moab, you were not alone."

We romanticize new beginnings, but the reality is that new beginnings feel a lot like dying. They involve grief. They involve confusion. They involve the humiliation of being a beginner again, not knowing the rules, feeling awkward, and asking for help.

You are suffering from the paralysis of analysis. What if I choose the wrong field? What if I move and I hate it? What if I never marry? What if I fail?

You are trying to write the end of the book while you are still in Chapter One. You are desperate for a ten-year plan because you think the plan will give you peace. You think, If God would just show me the roadmap, then I could rest.

But here is the hard truth: a map is not the same thing as a relationship. If you have a map, you do not need a guide. You can do it yourself. God rarely gives us maps. He gives us a lantern. A lantern only illuminates the next step. To see the step after that, you have to move. You have to stay close to the light.

The exhaustion of Ruth came from the vulnerability of being an outsider with no guarantee of safety. Your exhaustion comes from the vulnerability of not knowing if everything is going to be okay. You are lying on the threshing floor, in the dark, wondering if the Redeemer is going to wake up and cover you, or if you will be cast out into the cold.

THE RELEASE

Here is the beauty of the story of Ruth. It is a story of micro-obedience.

Ruth never had a big vision. She did not stand on the border of Moab and say, "I declare that I will go to Bethlehem, marry a wealthy landowner, become the great-grandmother of King David, and be one of only five women mentioned in the genealogy of Jesus Christ!"

She did not know any of that. She did not know about Boaz. She did not know about the lineage. She did not know she was being written into the greatest story ever told.

What did she know? She knew she had to stay with Naomi. That was the first step. She knew she had to walk to Bethlehem. That was the second. She knew she had to find food today. That was the third. She knew she had to listen to the instructions of Naomi about the threshing floor. That was the fourth.

That is it. She lived her life one stalk of barley at a time. She lived her life one courageous night at a time.

The release for you tonight is this: you do not need to know the ten-year plan. In fact, you could not handle it if you knew it. If God had told Ruth the whole story, that she would lose her husband, move to a country that hated her, be destitute, and have to propose to a stranger, she might have stayed in Moab out of fear. The mystery was a mercy.

Rest comes from obedience in the moment. Did you do the thing God asked you to do today? Did you send the email? Did you pack the box? Did you pray the prayer? Did you feed your children? Then you have succeeded.

The outcome is not your responsibility. The outcome belongs to Boaz, and Boaz represents God. When Ruth lay down at the feet of Boaz, she was saying, "I have done all I can do. I have come as far as I can walk. The rest is up to you."

And Boaz did not reject her. He woke up. He saw her. He covered her with the corner of his garment, which was a symbol of marriage and protection. He redeemed her. He gave her a home, a son, and a future she could never have imagined.

God is your family-redeemer. He knows you are in the dark. He knows you are on the threshing floor. He is not asleep. He is working out the details while you wait.

You are exhausted because you are trying to force a harvest before the seeds have even had time to sprout. You are throwing your weight against a door you were never meant to break down, instead of waiting for the Key-Holder to open it.

Release the need to know. Release the need to control the timeline. Embrace the lantern life. The light is enough for the step you are on. And that is all you need.

THE INVITATION

We spend so much time squinting at the horizon, trying to see the future, that we trip over the present. Tonight, we are going to change our focus. We are going to zoom in.

1. **The Horizon Check.** Close your eyes. Notice where your mind is wandering. Are you thinking about next month? Next year? Ten years from now? Say: "That is the horizon. I cannot touch it. I release it."
2. **The Zoom In.** Bring your focus closer. Bring it to this week. Then to tomorrow. Then to this very moment.
3. **The Question.** Ask God one simple question: "Lord, what is the one small thing You are asking of me for tomorrow?" Not: "What is my destiny?" Not: "Who will I marry?" Just: "What is the barley for tomorrow?"
4. **The Answer.** Listen for the small, simple answer. It might be: "Call your mom." It might be: "Apply for that one job." It might be: "Drink water and rest." It might be: "Be kind to the cashier."
5. **The Vow.** Commit to doing that one thing. That is your stalk of grain. Trust that if you pick up that one stalk, God will lead you to the next one.

You build a life the same way Ruth gathered a harvest: one small, faithful handful at a time.

BEDTIME PRAYER

The threshing floor is quiet. The stars are out over Bethlehem. You are lying at the feet of the One who holds your future. You do not need to be afraid of the dark. The Redeemer is here.

Whisper these words into the mystery.

God of Ruth, God of the Borderlands, God of the Fog,

I confess that I am exhausted by the unknown. I am tired of squinting into the future. I am tired of trying to be the architect of my own life. I am scared of making a mistake.

Tonight, I lay down my map. I admit that I cannot see the horizon. And I choose to believe that this is okay.

You are the family-redeemer. You know the way to Bethlehem. You know the field where I belong.

I will not worry about the harvest of next year. I will simply gather the grace for today. I will take the next small step. And I will trust You with the rest.

Cover me with Your garment. Hide me in Your plan. I am safe in the mystery.

Amen.

CONCLUSION

We have walked a long road together in these pages.

We have sat in the dust with Hagar. We have wept in the temple with Hannah. We have stood in the kitchen with Martha and waited on the threshing floor with Ruth. We have visited the waiting rooms, the deserts, and the dark nights of the soul.

Now, we arrive at the end. Or perhaps, we arrive at the beginning.

Throughout this book, we have talked about exhaustion as a problem to be solved, a burden to be lifted, or a wound to be healed. It is all of those things. But as we close this journey, I want to offer you a different perspective on your tiredness.

I want to suggest that your exhaustion is not just a symptom of a busy life. It is a signpost. It is a biological and spiritual alarm bell ringing in the center of your being, trying to remind you of your original design.

You are tired because you are fighting your own architecture. You are trying to be a machine in a world that was created to be a garden.

To understand why you need rest, and why you have permission to take it, we must go back to the very first story. Before the exhaustion of Hagar, before the striving of Leah, or the grief of Naomi, we have to go back to the moment when time began.

The First Sabbath

Imagine the rhythm of Creation.

The first chapter of Genesis is written like a song. It has a cadence, a beat, and a pulse. "And the evening and the morning were the first day. And the evening and the morning were the second day."

God speaks, and galaxies spin into the velvet dark. He whispers, and oceans gather around continents. He sculpts the mountains. He paints the sky. He fills the waters with living, swarming things and the air with winged birds. It is an explosion of productivity, work on a cosmic scale. By the end of the sixth day, God creates humanity. He looks at everything He has made and declares that it is very good.

Then the rhythm changes.

On the seventh day, God brings His work to a close, and He rests from everything He has made.

Stop and think about that for a moment. Does God have muscles that get sore? No. Does God have a mind that gets foggy? No. Does God run out of energy? No. The prophet Isaiah reminds us that the everlasting God, the Lord, the Creator of the ends of the earth, does not faint and does not grow weary.

So, if God was not tired, why did He rest?

He did not rest to recover. He did not rest to recharge His batteries so He could get back to work on Monday. He rested to enjoy.

He stopped creating so that He could start delighting. He stopped doing so that He could simply be with what He had made. He created a sanctuary in time: a palace of twenty-four hours where the only agenda was celebration, presence, and peace.

God blesses the seventh day and sets it apart. Do you realize this is the first thing in all of Scripture that God makes holy? Not a mountain. Not a temple. Not a person. Time.

Rest is holy.

This changes everything. For years, you may have viewed rest as a weakness. You thought rest was the penalty for being human. You thought: "I have to rest because I am limited, but if I were stronger, I could keep going."

But that is not the theology of Genesis. Rest is not a concession to weakness. Rest is a divine act. When you stop, when you put down your phone, when you close the laptop, when you sit on the porch and watch the sunset, or when you take a nap, you are not being lazy. You are being like God.

The Image of the Resting God

You were made in the Image of God. We usually talk about this in terms of our ability to create, to love, or to reason. But it also applies to our rhythm.

You were designed to work, yes. But you were also designed to stop. You were built with a Sabbath rhythm woven into your DNA. Your heart beats and rests. Your lungs inhale and exhale. The seasons turn from harvest to winter. The night follows the day.

But we have broken the rhythm. We live in a culture that worships the machine. A machine does not have a circadian rhythm. A machine does not need a Sabbath. A machine runs twenty-four hours a day until a gear snaps, and then you replace the part.

You have been trying to live like a machine. You have tried to override the off switch. You have treated sleep like an inconvenience. You have treated stillness like a waste of time. You have convinced yourself that if you are not producing, you do not exist.

Your soul is screaming. Your exhaustion is the friction of a human soul trying to live at the pace of a machine.

But here is the good news: you can stop. You can stop because the work is already finished.

In the Old Testament, the Sabbath was a reminder that the people were no longer slaves in Egypt. In Egypt, there were no days off. Pharaoh never said: "Take a break." Slaves work until they die. When God gave the commandment to Sabbath, He was saying: "You are not slaves. You are free. Only free people can choose to stop."

In the New Testament, Jesus takes it even further. On the cross, His final words were: "It is finished." The work of redemption is done. The striving of Leah is over. The guilt of the Samaritan woman is washed away. The debt is paid.

You do not have to work to save yourself. You do not have to work to earn the love of God. You do not have to work to justify your space on this planet.

You can rest, not because you have finished your to-do list, for you never will, but because He has finished the work that matters.

The Sabbath of the Heart

As you close this book, I am not asking you to follow a rigid set of rules. I am not asking you to become a legalist about your schedule.

I am inviting you into the Sabbath of the Heart.

This is an internal posture. It is a portable sanctuary that you can carry with you into the noise of your life. It is the quiet confidence that says: "I am not what I do. I am not what I earn. I am not what I produce. I am a daughter of the King, and He delights in me even when I am doing absolutely nothing."

It is the permission to leave the dishes in the sink because you need to hold your child. It is the permission to say no to the extra committee so you can say yes to your sanity. It is the permission to turn off the news because the world is for God to manage, not you. It is the permission to sleep.

Remember the women we met? Hagar found rest when she realized she was seen. Hannah found rest when she poured out her soul. Ruth found rest when she lay at the feet of the Redeemer. Mary found rest when she released her son to the Father. The bleeding woman found rest when she stopped hiding.

They did not find rest by working harder. They found rest by surrendering. They found rest by admitting they were human and letting God be God.

You are safe to do the same.

A Final Prayer

The sun has gone down. The day is over. You do not have to carry the world anymore. Let the shoulders drop. Let the jaw unclench. Let the mind drift.

Receive this blessing as you go to sleep.

> *To the woman who is tired in her bones: may you find the deep, heavy sleep of the beloved. May the racing thoughts in your mind be silenced by the steady rhythm of grace. May you realize that the world will keep spinning while you sleep, held by hands much stronger than yours.*
>
> *To the woman who feels she has not done enough: may you hear the whisper of the Creator saying: "it was very good." May you know that your worth is not in the harvest you gathered, but in the fact that you are His. May you drop the rope of striving and fall into the net of love.*
>
> *To the woman who is hurting: may the God of Hagar see you. May the God of Elijah feed you. May the God of the widow sustain you.*

You have permission to rest. You have permission to be small. You have permission to be human.

Goodnight, daughter. All is well. All is well.

Amen.

YOUR WORDS MATTER

Help another exhausted woman find rest

Now that you have spent time in these stories, I hope you feel a little more steady, a little more seen, and a little less alone.

If you are willing, would you leave an honest review?

Your review helps other exhausted women find a book that offers Scripture without pressure, comfort without performance, and a place to breathe when they are running on empty. Your words could be the reason someone takes a first small step toward rest, or opens these pages on a night when she does not know what else to do.

Thank you for being part of this journey. By sharing your experience, you help keep this kind of gentle, permission-giving encouragement within reach for the women who need it most.

With gratitude,

Zoe Lamb